A CONCISE
COPTIC-ENGLISH LEXICON
Second Edition

SOCIETY OF BIBLICAL LITERATURE
Resources for Biblical Study

Edited by
Beverly Gaventa

Number 35
A CONCISE
COPTIC-ENGLISH LEXICON
Second Edition

by
Richard Smith

A CONCISE
COPTIC-ENGLISH LEXICON
Second Edition

by
Richard Smith

Society of Biblical Literature
Atlanta

A CONCISE
COPTIC-ENGLISH LEXICON
Second Edition

by
Richard Smith

Copyright © 1983 by Richard Smith
Revisions copyright © 1999 by the Society of Biblical Literature

Typesetting by Richard Whitaker on an HP LaserJet II P
and an Ibycus SC Computer.
Coptic and Greek fonts designed by and software written by Richard Whitaker.
Reprinted in paperback by the Society of Biblical Literature, 2000.

Library of Congress Cataloging-in-Publication Data

Smith, Richard, 1943 Sept. 28–
    A concise Coptic-English lexicon / by Richard H. Smith. — 2nd ed.
        p.   cm. — (Resources for biblical study ; no. 35)
    Includes bibliographical references.
    ISBN 0-7885-0561-0 (cloth : alk. paper)
    ISBN 0-88414-039-3 (paper : alk. paper)
    1. Coptic language Dictionaries—English.   I. Title. II. Series.
PJ2181.S63   1999
493'.2321—dc21   99-27936
                                                   CIP

08 07 06 05 04 03 02 01 00   5 4 3 2
Printed in the United States of America
on acid-free paper

TABLE OF CONTENTS

PREFACE TO THE SECOND EDITION

In the years since its publication, this lexicon has served well as a classroom tool. Over the years, however, reviewers and colleagues have pointed out errors and suggested improvements, and I am grateful to Scholars Press, in republishing the book, for allowing me to incorporate most of these suggestions. Hardly a page has been left without some refinement. I will discuss some more general matters in this preface.

The transliterations of the letters have provoked comment, but they are from the system recommended by the Society of Biblical Literature's "Instructions for Contributors." The names of the letters are from late manuscripts, often in the Bohairic dialect, and are given simply for their usefulness.

In the year this lexicon was first published, a popular introductory grammar of the language also appeared (Lambdin, 1983), but for an overview of the grammar more consistent with this lexicon, see Emmel, 1992 (which contains a good bibliography of Coptology), and the forthcoming grammar of Bentley Layton. The Bibliography of this lexicon ("Resources") remains a list of sources used in its compilation.

Much unpublished Nag Hammadi material that I had access to over a decade ago is now published in the E. J. Brill series of editions with Coptic indexes. The French language editions, in the series *Bibliothèque Copte de Nag Hammadi,* published by the University of Laval, is, as of 1992, being accompanied by complete computer generated concordances to each codex.

On the publication of this second edition I would like to thank my students from over the years, who challenged nearly every entry in its pages. Also, once again, thanks to Richard Whitaker not only for typesetting, but for designing Coptic fonts. Finally, I want to thank the Society of Biblical Literature for awarding this project a research grant which helped prepare the manuscript for publication.

Richard H. Smith
Claremont Graduate University
Institute for Antiquity and Christianity

PREFACE TO THE FIRST EDITION

This small Coptic lexicon has its origin in a word list compiled for students. The unavailability of a student dictionary had presented an obstacle to the teaching of the language. The work thus grew out of a classroom setting. It is intended primarily for beginners, yet its handy size may also make it a useful reference for advanced readers. Several colleagues, also faced with the need for such a book, encouraged its publication.

Coptology is fortunate to have among its tools one of the finest of ancient language dictionaries, that by W. E. Crum. Crum's dictionary is essential for understanding the meanings of Coptic words. The student is discouraged from using this concise lexicon to the exclusion of Crum, especially as he or she progresses. Crum's dictionary, unfortunately, is convenient in neither size nor price. The present dictionary is designed to be both handy and affordable. During the years since Crum's great work was published, a few minor corrections have been made to the placement or understanding of certain words. Where I am aware of these, I have taken them into account.

In compiling this lexicon I received helpful suggestions, specific and general, from many scholars. I thank them all, especially Stephen Emmel. All final decisions, however, including those found to be erroneous, are my own. For the design and technical production of the book, I am grateful to Richard Whitaker. Two of my students have been indispensible. Frans Huizenga helped prepare the manuscript for publication and Deborah Ellens performed the rigorous task of putting it into the computer. Finally, I would like to give my deeply felt thanks to James M. Robinson and the staff of the Institute for Antiquity and Christianity in Claremont, California, -- James Brashler, James Goehring and Marvin Meyer. They not only assisted with this project but also gave enduring encouragement to my studies.
ⲁⲩⲱ ⲁⲓ̈ⲣ̄ⲙⲡϣⲁ ⲉⲃⲟⲗ ϩⲓⲧⲟⲟⲧⲟⲩ (NH VII,118:21-22)

INTRODUCTION

USING THE LEXICON

The words are alphabetized, as in Crum's dictionary, primarily by root consonants and then by the vowels within the structure of consonants. A glance down the first dozen or so words under в, for example, should make the system clear. Words having an initial vowel are alphabetized by that vowel and then by the consonantal root. This system is practical because the root of a Coptic word is its consonants. Thus all forms, derivatives and variant spellings can be placed under one main entry. Since a primary concern of this lexicon is to be helpful to students, many forms that are difficult to recognize are cross-listed, a brief definition is given, and the abbreviation v. directs attention to the main entry. Most forms resulting simply from vowel reduction have not been cross-listed. Therefore, many prenominal and presuffixal forms beginning with a short vowel can be found under a longer vowel: for оп⸗ look up ωπ. In Nag Hammadi texts, the о sometimes shifts to ⲁ, thus for ⲁп⸗ look up ωπ.

Since Coptic and English belong to different language families, and Coptic words are not always described by the word class of their English translation, this lexicon usually avoids giving parts of speech. With substantives, the gender is an important consideration in translating, and this is noted m. (masculine) or f. (feminine). When the gender is not known, this lexicon simply indicates n. (noun). An adjectival definition following a noun usually relates to the use of that noun in an attributive relationship. Any Coptic infinitive can be used as a masculine noun. In this lexicon, where the nominal definitions are given, they are separated from the verbal definitions by a semicolon.

Many compound nouns with such common prefixes as ⲁⲧ-, ⲙⲛⲧ-, ⲣⲙ, ⲣⲉϥ-, and ϭⲓⲛ- are not listed in this lexicon, nor are many of the compound verbs formed with such words as ⲕⲁ-, ⲣ-, ϯ-, ϣⲡ-, ϭⲓ-, and ϫⲓ-. The lexicon does, however, contain all of the compounds listed by Bruce Metzger as occurring frequently in the Coptic New Testament.

Many grammatical forms are given in the lexicon which may be especially helpful to beginners. The proper translation of such material is determined by context. It is included here more as a convenience than as a guide. I assume that this book will be used in conjunction with the study of grammar.

In the interest of simplicity, the lexicon is not exhaustive with regard to variants in spelling. Words spelled with ï, for instance, may also be spelled with єι, and vice versa. Likewise, γ and oγ sometimes interchange. The use of supralinear strokes is limited to the sonants в, λ, м, n, and ρ. Actual scribal systems of supralineation varied from manuscript to manuscript.

GREEK WORDS IN COPTIC

A complete Coptic vocabulary properly includes many words derived from Greek. A dictionary of this vocabulary has never been ventured, though it is greatly needed. In reading Coptic texts, one must work with a Greek lexicon and suffer the problems that arise from partial assimilation of the words to the Coptic language. A few, indeed, have found their way directly into Coptic dictionaries, e.g., вλλoт from μηλωτή. However, since most Greek derivatives are not included in Coptic dictionaries, a few remarks on their nature might be helpful.

Greek adjectives are used in Coptic as nouns. Nouns derived from Greek retain their masculine or feminine gender. As there is no Coptic neuter, neuter nouns become masculine. Verbs derived from Greek tend to appear in the Greek present imperative form. In all dialects but Sahidic, and frequently in the Nag Hammadi texts, these verbs require the Coptic auxiliar verb ρ̄- (from єιρє *do*).

Greek words may appear in Coptic in non-classical Greek spellings. For the Greek rough breathing, Coptic tends to use 2, but will sometimes also use this letter to aspirate words that, in Greek, have a smooth breathing: 2ικωn for єἰκών. Non-classical manuscripts may employ unexpected aspiration, so that in the version of *The Apocryphon of John* in Nag Hammadi Codex III we find 2ιμλρμєnн, in the Codex II version ωιμλρμєnн, and in the Codex IV version χιμλρμєnн for єἱμαρμένη.

A few Greek words developed Coptic forms: ψγχooγє and гρλφooγє as the plurals *souls* and *scriptures*. Κατά and παρά developed the presuffixal forms κλτλρo⸗ and πλρλρo⸗. Coptic texts use the standard Greek abbreviations for sacred names such as τ̄c̄ for Ἰησοῦς. A list of these is given in most of the grammars.

THE NAG HAMMADI CODICES

A single archaeological event is responsible for most of the recent interest in Coptic studies: the discovery in 1945 of a collection of Gnostic texts near Nag Hammadi, Egypt. Because of the importance of these texts, the publisher encouraged the compiler of this lexicon to make it more useful for Nag Hammadi reading. Doing this required certain format decisions that have to be explained. Most Coptic teaching and reference materials describe the classical Sahidic dialect of the language. The texts of the Coptic-Gnostic library show us a rather inchoate stage of the language. Codices I, X, and the first two tractates of Codex XI are primarily in the Subachmimic dialect. The bulk of the Nag Hammadi Library gives the general appearance of Sahidic, yet betrays characteristics of Subachmimic and occasionally dialects spoken even further down the Nile, Fayyumic and Bohairic. Moreover, certain words and characteristics labeled by Crum as "archaic" or "older MSS" appear in the Nag

Hammadi texts. Many words and spellings that appear in the Nag Hammadi texts were previously unattested.

The most notable of the features differing from standard Sahidic are several shifts among the vowels, primarily ⲁ for ⲟ, ⲁ for ⲉ, and ⲉ for ⲁ. ï is frequently written ⲉⲓ following vowels. Double vowels can become single, and single vowels double. A final ⲉ is sometimes added after a consonant. The supralinear stroke can be used to indicate ⲉ (ⲑⲛ̄- for the plural indefinite article ⲑⲉⲛ-, occasionally in the possessive articles ⲡⲛ̄-, etc.). ⲛ̄- can be assimilated to ⲣ (ⲣ̄ⲣⲱⲙⲉ) or ⲃ (ⲃ̄ⲃⲗⲁⲉ). The full form of a verb can be used as a prenominal form. ⲣ̄- is often used as an auxiliary with Greek verbs. ⲛ̄- sometimes appears before Greek conjunctions: ⲛ̄ⲅⲁⲣ, ⲛ̄ⲁⲉ, ⲙ̄ⲙⲉⲛ.

This lexicon is fundamentally a Sahidic lexicon. All material not considered by Crum to be standard Sahidic has been bracketed. Also bracketed are a few words labeled Sahidic by Crum but whose attestation appears confined to the Coptic Gnostic corpus, e.g. ⲡⲱϣ̄ϥ. Not every spelling variant is listed. Most conjectural readings and some *hapax legomena* have been excluded. Nonetheless, the words listed provide a large enough vocabulary for the reading of Nag Hammadi texts along with standard texts such as the Coptic New Testament.

Enclosure of material in brackets is not a statement about Coptic dialects. It should be understood that there is no Nag Hammadi dialect, nor is there much consistency in dialect from codex to codex nor often even from tractate to tractate. The coming years will see the continued study of the language in which these texts are written. Doubtless a definitive treatment, perhaps even a revision of Crum's dictionary, will result. In the meantime, I hope this modest book encourages the reading of Nag Hammadi texts by those whose interest is not primarily linguistic but rather the appreciation and interpretation of these most intriguing documents.

RESOURCES

Böhlig, Alexander, and Wisse, Frederik, eds. *Nag Hammadi Codices III,2 and IV,2: The Gospel of the Egyptians.* Leiden: E. J. Brill, 1975.

Crum, W. E. *A Coptic Dictionary.* Oxford: Clarendon Press, 1939.

Černý, J. *Coptic Etymological Dictionary.* Cambridge: University Press, 1976.

Draguet, René. *Index Copte et Grec-Copte de la Concordance du nouveau Testament Sahidique.* Louvain, 1960.

Emmel, Stephen. *Nag Hammadi Codex II,2-7*, 2 vols. (Bentley Layton, ed.). Indexes. Leiden: E. J. Brill, 1989.

Emmel, Stephen. *Nag Hammadi Codex III,5, The Dialogue of the Savior.* Leiden: E. J. Brill, 1984.

Emmel, Stephen. "Coptic Language." In D. N. Freedman, ed. *The Anchor Bible Dictionary*, vol. 4. New York: Doubleday, 1992.

Hedrick, Charles W. *Nag Hammadi Codices XI, XII and XIII.* Leiden: E. J. Brill, 1990.

Kasser, R., *et al.*, eds. *Tractatus Tirpartitus*, 2 vols. Bern: Francke, 1973-75.

Krause, Martin and Girgis, Viktor. "Neue Texte" (Nag Hammadi Codex VII, *1, 2, 3,* and *5*). In Altheim, Franz and Stiehl, Ruth, eds. *Christenturm am Roten Meer*, vol. 2. Berlin: Walter de Gruyter, 1973.

Krause, Martin and Labib, Pahor. *Die Drei Versionen Des Apokryphon Des Johannes im Koptischen Museum zu Alt-Kairo.* Wiesbaden: Otto Harrassowitz, 1962.

Lambdin, Thomas O. *Introduction to Sahidic Coptic.* Macon: Mercer, 1983.

Layton, Bentley. *A Coptic Grammar.* Unpublished.

Layton, Bentley. *The Gnostic Treatise on Resurrection from Nag Hammadi.* Missoula: Scholars Press, 1979.

Layton, Bentley. "The Hypostasis of the Archons," *Harvard Theological Review* 67 (1974), 351-425: 69 (1976), 31-101.

Malinine, M., *et al.*, eds *Epistula Iacobi Apocrypha.* Zurich: Rascher, 1968.

Malinine, M., *et al.*, eds. *Evangelium Veritatis.* Zurich: Rascher, 1956.

Metzger, Bruce M. *Lists of Words Occuring Frequently in the Coptic New Testament.* Grand Rapids: William B. Eerdmans, 1962.

Meyer, Marvin W. *The Letter of Peter to Philip.* Missoula: Scholars Press, 1981.

Parrott, Douglas M. ed. *Nag Hammadi Codices III,3-4 and V,1 with BG 8502,3.* Leiden: E. J. Brill, 1991.

Parrott, Douglas M. ed. *Nag Hammadi Codices V,2-5 and VI with Papyrus Berolinensis 8502, 1* and *4.* Leiden: E. J. Brill, 1979.

Pearson, Birger A., ed. *Nag Hammadi Codex VII.* Leiden: E. J. Brill, 1996.

Pearson, Birger A., ed. *Nag Hammadi Codices IX and X.* Leiden: E. J. Brill, 1981.

Plumley, J. Martin. *An Introductory Coptic Grammar (Sahidic Dialect).* London: Home and Van Thal, 1948.

Sieber, John. *Nag Hammadi Codex VIII.* Leiden: E. J. Brill, 1991.

Till, Walter C. *Koptische Grammatik (saïdischer Dialekt) mit Bibliographie, Lesestücken und Wörterverzeichnissen.* Leipzig: VEB, 1961.

Turner, John D. *The Book of Thomas the Contender.* Missoula: Scholars Press, 1975

Waldstein, Michael, and Wisse, Frederik, *The Apocryphon of John: Synopsis of Nag Hammadi: Codices II,1; III, 1; and IV, 1 with BG 8502, 2.* Leiden: E. J. Brill, 1996.

Westendorf, Wolfhart. *Koptisches Handwörterbuch.* Heidelberg: Carl Winter, 1977.

ABBREVIATIONS AND SIGNS

art.	article
aux.	auxiliary
caus.	causative verb
cf.	*confer* (compare the entry indicated)
conj. base	conjugation base (tense marker)
def.	definite
f. or fem.	feminine
Gk.	Greek
imper.	imperative form of verb
indef.	indefinite
m. or masc.	masculine
n.	noun (with no attested gender)
neg.	negative
p.c.	*paticipium conjunctum* (conjunctive particle)
pl.	plural
q.v.	*quod vide* (which see)
sing.	singular
subj.	subject
v.	*vide* (see the word indicated for the proper entry)
vb.	verb
-	prenominal form
⸍	presuffixal form
†	qualitative form of verb
;	separates verbal and nominal definitions
( )	Parenthetical comments amplify usage or relate to derivation.
[ ]	Brackets contain words, forms and definitions found in Nag Hammadi texts that Crum does not consider standard Sahidic Coptic.

ⲁ
called ⲁⲗⲫⲁ   transliterated *a*

ⲁ̅   as number *one*

[ⲁ   can stand in place of ⲉ or ⲟ]

ⲁ̸ [ⲁ⳿ⲁ̸], ⲁ- conjugation base I perfect (from ⲉⲓⲣⲉ)

ⲁ- prefix of imperative (some vbs.)

[ⲁ-, ⲁⲣⲁ̸] v. ⲉ-, ⲉⲣⲟ̸   *to, for*

ⲁ-, ⲛⲁ- *about, approximately* (used with distance, weight, numbers and time)

ⲁⲁ̸ v. ⲉⲓⲣⲉ *do, make*

ⲁⲓⲁⲓ [ⲁⲉⲓⲉⲩ], ⲟⲓⲧ [ⲁⲉⲓⲧ] *increase, grow, be great†, honored†; m. increase, growth*

  ⲁⲉⲓⲏⲥ [ⲁⲉⲓⲏ, ⲁⲙⲁⲉⲓⲏ] f. *size*

ⲁⲓⲱ v. ⳿ⲁⲓⲟ   *hail!*

ⲁⲃⲱ   f. *net*

ⲁⲃⲱⲕ, pl. ⲁⲃⲟⲟⲕⲉ   m. *crow, raven*

[ⲁⲉⲓⲃ̅ⲧⲉ] v. ⲉⲓⲉⲃⲧ   *east*

ⲁⲃⲁϭⲏⲉⲓⲛ, ⳿ⲁⲃⲁϭⲏⲉⲓⲛ   m.f. *glass*

ⲁⲉⲓⲕ   m. *consecration*

  ϫⲓⲁⲉⲓⲕ   *consecrate; m. consecration*

ⲁⲕⲏⲥ   m. *belt, apron*

ⲁⲗ   n. *deaf, hearing impaired person*

ⲁⲗ   m. *pebble, stone*

  ⲁⲗⲙ̅ⲡⲉ   *hail stone*

ⲁⲗⲉ, ⲁⲗⲟ̸, ⲁⲗⲏⲩ†, imper. ⲁⲗⲱⲧⲛ̅   *mount, go up, ascend*

ⲁⲗⲟ̸   *stop!* (imper. of ⲗⲟ)

ⲁⲗⲟⲩ [ⲉⲗⲟⲩ]   m.f. *child, boy, girl*

  ⲁⲗⲱ [ⲉⲗⲟⲩ]   f. *pupil* of eye

ⲁⲗⲱ, ⲉⲗⲱ, pl. ⲁⲗⲟⲟⲩⲉ   f. *snare, trap*

ⲁⲗⲧⲕⲁⲥ [ⲁⲧⲕⲁⲥ]   m. *marrow*

ⲁⲙⲟⲩ, 2nd person sing. fem. ⲁⲙⲏ, 2nd person pl. ⲁⲙⲏⲓⲛ, ⲁⲙⲏⲉⲓⲧⲛ̅, ⲁⲙⲱⲓⲛⲉ [ⲁⲙⲏⲧⲛ̅]   *come!* (imper. of ⲉⲓ)

ⲁⲙⲛ̅ⲧⲉ [ⲉⲙⲛ̅ⲧⲉ]   m. *hell, hades, the underworld*

ⲁⲙⲣ̅ϩⲉ   m. *asphalt*

ⲁⲙⲁϩⲧⲉ [ⲉⲙⲁϩⲧⲉ]   *prevail, grab, rule, detain; m. power, might*

  ⲁⲧⲁⲙⲁϩⲧⲉ   *uncontrollable, incomprehensible*

ⲁⲛ- *great one of, commander* prefixed to certain numerals and nouns

ⲁⲛ-, pl. ⲁⲛⲁⲛ- collective numeral prefix

ⲁⲛ [ⲉⲛ] postpositive negative particle *not*

ⲁⲛ- *we* (ⲁⲛⲟⲛ)

1

[ⲁⲛ] v. ⲟⲛ *again*

ⲁⲛⲁⲓ̈, ⲁⲛⲓⲧ† *be pleasing, pleasant;* m. *beauty*
  ⲣ̄ⲁⲛⲁ⸗ [ⲣ̄ⲉⲛⲁ⸗] *be pleasing to, please*

ⲁⲛⲟⲕ, ⲁⲛⲅ- personal pronoun 1st person sing. m.f. *I (am)*
  ⲁⲛⲟⲕ [ⲁⲛⲁⲕ], ⲁⲛⲅ- *I*
  ⲛ̄ⲧⲟⲕ [ⲛ̄ⲧⲁⲕ], ⲛ̄ⲧⲕ- *you sing. masc.*
  ⲛ̄ⲧⲟ, ⲛ̄ⲧⲉ- *you sing. fem.*
  ⲛ̄ⲧⲟϥ [ⲛ̄ⲧⲁϥ] *he*
  ⲛ̄ⲧⲟⲥ [ⲛ̄ⲧⲁⲥ] *she*
  ⲁⲛⲟⲛ [ⲁⲛⲁⲛ], ⲁⲛ- *we*
  ⲛ̄ⲧⲱⲧⲛ̄ [ⲛ̄ⲧⲱⲧⲛⲉ], ⲛ̄ⲧⲉⲧⲛ̄- *you pl.*
  ⲛ̄ⲧⲟⲟⲩ [ⲛ̄ⲧⲁⲩ] *they*

ⲁⲛⲉⲓⲛⲉ, ⲁⲛⲓ⸗ *bring!* (imper. of ⲉⲓⲛⲉ)

ⲁⲛⲥⲏⲃⲉ, ⲁⲛⲍⲏⲃⲉ f. *school*

ⲁⲛⲥⲙ̄ⲙⲉ *ordinance* v. ⲥⲙ̄ⲙⲉ

ⲁⲛⲁⲩ *look!* (imper. of ⲛⲁⲩ)

ⲁⲛⲁϣ [ⲁⲛⲟϣ, ⲉⲛⲁϣ], pl. ⲁⲛⲁⲩϣ m. *oath*
  ⲣ̄ⲁⲛⲁϣ *swear*

[ⲁⲛⲏϩⲉ] v. ⲉⲛⲉϩ *eternity*

ⲁⲛⲭⲱⲝ *chief* v. ⲭⲱⲝ

ⲁⲡⲁ title of respect for monks and saints (ἀββά)

ⲁⲡⲉ, pl. ⲁⲡⲏⲩⲉ f. *head, chief, authority*

ⲁⲡⲣⲏⲧⲉ f. *period of time, while, briefly*

ⲁⲡⲥ [ⲁⲯ], ⲏⲡⲥ f. *number* (ⲱⲡ)

ⲁⲡⲟⲧ m. *cup*

ⲁⲣⲓ-, ⲁⲣⲓ⸗ *do!* (imper. of ⲉⲓⲣⲉ)

ⲁⲣⲏⲃ m. *pledge, deposit*

ⲁⲣⲓⲕⲉ m. *blame, accusation*
  ϭⲛ̄ⲁⲣⲓⲕⲉ ⲉ- *blame, find fault with*

ⲁⲣⲓⲣⲉ, ⲁⲣⲓ-, ⲁⲣⲓ⸗ *do!* (imper. of ⲉⲓⲣⲉ)

ⲁⲣⲏⲩ *perhaps, if,* or forming an interrogative

ⲁⲣⲟⲟⲩⲉ n. *thistle*

ⲁⲣⲟϣ *become cold;* m. *cold*

ⲁⲣϣⲓⲛ m. *lentil, lentil soup*

ⲁⲣⲉϩ [ⲁⲣⲏϩ] v. ϩⲁⲣⲉϩ *keep*

[ⲁⲣⲉⲭ†] v. ⲱⲣⲝ *be firm*

ⲁⲣⲏϫ⸗ n. *end of, boundary of, limit of*

ⲁⲥ [ⲉⲥ] *old*

ⲁⲁⲥ in ϯⲁⲁⲥ *punch, hit, slap*

ⲁⲥⲁⲓ̈ [ⲉⲥⲓⲉⲉⲓ], ⲁⲥⲱⲟⲩ†, ⲁⲥⲓⲱⲟⲩ† [ⲁⲥⲓⲏⲟⲩⲧ†, ⲉⲥⲓⲱⲟⲩⲧ†] *be light, relieved, swift*
  ϩⲛ̄ⲟⲩⲁⲥⲁⲓ̈ *lightly*

-ⲁⲥⲉ v. ⲥⲟⲟⲩ *six*

[ⲁⲥⲉ, ⲁⲥⲓ] v. ⲟⲥⲉ *loss*

ⲁⲥⲡⲉ f. *language, speech*

ⲁⲥⲟⲩ [ⲉⲥⲟⲩ] f. *price, value*

[ⲁⲥϩ] *sickle* v. ⲱϩⲥ

ⲁⲧ- negative particle *not, without, un-, in-, -less*

[ⲁⲧⲉ] v. ⲟⲟⲧⲉ *womb*

ⲁⲧⲟ, ⲁⲧⲉ- n. *crowd, many, various*
   ⲁⲧⲉⲥⲙⲟⲧ *variety*
[ⲁⲧⲕⲁⲥ] v. ⲁⲁⲧⲕⲁⲥ *marrow*
ⲁⲩ, ⲁⲩⲓ, ⲁⲩⲉⲓⲥ *come!, give!, hand over!*
ⲁⲩ- (for ⲁⲟⲩ with ⲟ eliding) I perfect before indef. art. sing.
[ⲁⲩ-] v. ⲉⲩ-
ⲁⲩⲱ *and,* coordinates phrases or nouns, cf. ⲙⲛ̄-, ϩⲓ-
   ⲁⲩⲱ ⲟⲛ *moreover*
ⲁⲩⲁⲛ, ⲁⲩⲁⲁⲛ, ⲁⲩⲉⲓⲛ [ⲉⲟⲩⲁⲛ] m. *color, appearance*
ⲁⲩⲱⲛ *open!* (imper. of ⲟⲩⲱⲛ)
ⲁⲩⲏⲧ m. *company, crowd,* monastic *community*
ⲁϣ [ⲉϣ] *what?, who?, which?*
   ⲁϣ ⲛ̄ϩⲉ, ⲛ̄ⲁϣ ⲛ̄ϩⲉ *how?*
ⲁϣⲁⲓ̈ [ⲁϣⲉⲓ̈, ⲁϣⲉⲉⲓⲧⲉ], ⲟⲩⲁϯ *become many, multiply;* m. *multitude*
   ⲁϣⲏ f. *multitude*
ⲁϣⲉⲧ, ⲁϣⲧⲫ v. ⲉⲓϣⲉ *hang*
ⲁϣⲕⲁⲕ (ⲉⲃⲟⲗ) *call out* v. ϣⲕⲁⲕ
ⲁϥ m. *meat, flesh*
ⲁϥ m. *fly*
[ⲁϥⲧⲫ] v. ⲱϥⲧ *nail*
-ⲁϥⲧⲉ v. ϥⲧⲟⲟⲩ *four*
[ⲁϩⲫ] v. ⲁⲫ conj. base I perfect
ⲁϩⲉⲧ v. ⲱϩⲉ *stand*
ⲁϩⲉ m. *lifetime*
   ⲣ̄ⲁϩⲉ *spend a life*
ⲁϩⲉ v. ⲉϩⲉ *yes*
ⲁϩⲟ [ⲉϩⲟ], pl. ⲁϩⲱⲱⲣ [ⲉϩⲱⲣ] m. *treasure, storehouse, treasury*
ⲁϩⲟⲙ [ⲉϩⲟⲙ] in ⲁϣⲁϩⲟⲙ, ϥⲓⲁϩⲟⲙ *sigh, groan;* m. *groan*
ⲁϩⲱⲙ m. *eagle, falcon*
   ⲡⲁϩⲱⲙ name of early fourth-century founder of cenobitic monasticism,
   Pachomius
ⲁϩⲣⲟⲫ *what?, why?, what's wrong?*
ⲁϩⲉⲣⲁⲧⲫ v. ⲱϩⲉ *stand*
ⲁⲭⲓⲫ *speak!, say!* (imper. of ⲭⲱ)
ⲁⲭⲛ̄- [ⲁⲧⲭⲛⲉ-], ⲉⲭⲛ̄-, ⲁⲭⲛ̄ⲧⲫ, ⲉⲭⲛ̄ⲧⲫ *without*
ⲁϭⲃⲉⲥ, ⲁⲧⲃⲉⲥ f. *moisture*
ⲁϭⲣⲏⲛ f. *barren woman*

B

called ⲃⲏⲧⲁ   transliterated b

ⲃ̄ as number *two*
ⲃ sometimes interchanges with ϥ
[ⲃ̄- can stand for ⲛ̄-]
ⲃⲁ, ⲃⲁⲉ m. *palm branch*
ⲃⲱ v. ϥⲱ *hair*
ⲃⲱ ⲛ̄- [ⲃⲉ-ⲛ̄-] f. *-plant, -tree*
ⲃⲏⲃ m. *cave, hole, den, nest*

ⲃⲁⲁⲃⲉ, ⲃⲁⲃⲱⲱ⸗, p.c. ⲃⲁⲃⲉ- *be insipid, foolish, despise*
ⲃⲁⲃⲉⲣⲱⲙⲉ n. *braggart*
ⲃⲉⲉⲃⲉ, ⲃⲉⲃⲉ *bubble, pour, rain*
ⲃ̄ⲃⲣⲏϭⲉ v. ⲉⲃⲣⲏϭⲉ *lightning*
ⲃⲱⲕ, ⲃⲟⲕ⸗, ⲃⲏⲕ† *go, depart, be going*†
ⲃⲱⲕ ⲉⲃⲟⲗ *leave*
ⲃⲱⲕ ⲉⲡⲉⲥⲏⲧ *descend*
ⲃⲱⲕ ⲉϩⲣⲁï *ascend*
ⲃⲱⲕ ⲉϩⲟⲩⲛ (ⲉ-) *enter*
[ⲃⲱⲕ, f. ⲃⲱⲕⲓ, pl. ⲉⲃⲓⲁⲓⲕ, ⲃⲁⲓⲁⲓⲕ m. *servant, slave*]
ⲃⲉⲕⲉ, pl. ⲃⲉⲕⲏⲩⲉ m. *wage, payment, reward*
[ⲃⲟⲕⲓ n. *conception*
ⲉⲣⲃⲁⲕⲓ *become pregnant, make pregnant*
ⲃⲉⲕⲉ n. *fetus*]
ⲃⲁⲗ [ⲃⲉⲗ] m. *eye*
ⲃⲟⲗ [ⲃⲁⲗ] m. *outside*
ⲉⲃⲟⲗ [ⲁⲃⲟⲗ, ⲁⲃⲁⲗ] *out, outward, away*
ⲉⲃⲟⲗ ϩⲛ̄-, ⲛ̄ϩⲏⲧ⸗ *from, out of, as a result of*
ⲉⲃⲟⲗ ϫⲉ- *because*
ⲛ̄ⲃⲗ̄-, ⲛ̄ⲃⲗ̄ⲗⲁ⸗ *except*
ⲥⲁⲃⲟⲗ, ⲛ̄ⲥⲁⲃⲟⲗ, ⲛ̄ⲥⲁⲛ̄ⲃⲟⲗ *outside, beyond*
ϣⲁⲃⲟⲗ *to the end, forever*
ϩⲁⲃⲟⲗ *from, away from*
ϩⲓⲃⲟⲗ *outside*
ⲣ̄ⲃⲟⲗ *escape, flee*
ⲕⲁⲃⲟⲗ *vomit*
ⲃⲱⲗ, ⲃⲗ̄-, ⲃⲟⲗ⸗, ⲃⲁⲗ⸗, ⲃⲏⲗ†, p.c. ⲃⲁⲗ- *loosen, release, solve, interpret;* m. *interpretation*
ⲃⲱⲗ ⲉⲃⲟⲗ *release, destroy, dissolve, be ruined*†
ⲃⲟⲗⲃⲗ̄ [ⲃⲁⲗⲃⲗⲉ], ⲃⲗⲃⲱⲗ⸗, p.c. ⲃⲁⲗⲃⲗ̄- *dig up*
ⲃⲗ̄ⲃⲓⲗⲉ f. *kernel, seed, fruit, berry*
[ⲃⲱⲗⲕ, ⲃⲁⲗⲕ⸗, ⲃⲟⲗⲉⲕ† *be angry;* m. *anger*
ⲃⲗ̄ⲕⲉ f. *anger*]
ⲃⲗ̄ⲗⲉ [ⲃⲉⲗⲗⲏ], f. ⲃⲗ̄ⲗⲏ, pl. ⲃⲗ̄ⲗⲉⲉⲩⲉ [ⲃⲗ̄ⲗⲁⲁⲩ] m. *blind person*
ⲃⲁⲗⲟⲧ f. *sheepskin garment* (μηλωτή)
ⲃⲗ̄ϫⲉ, ⲃⲗ̄ⲗϫⲉ f. *pottery, shard*
ⲃⲁⲁⲙⲡⲉ m.f. *goat*
ⲃⲱⲱⲛ *bad, evil*
ⲃⲟⲟⲛⲉ f. *evil*
ⲉⲓⲉⲣⲃⲟⲟⲛⲉ f. *evil eye* (ⲉⲓⲁ)
ⲃⲛ̄ⲛⲉ f. *date palm, date*
ⲃⲉⲛⲓⲡⲉ [ⲃⲁⲛⲓⲡⲉ, ⲡⲉⲛⲓⲡⲉ] m. *iron, metal tool, sword, chain*
ⲃⲓⲣ, f. ⲃⲓⲣⲉ m. *basket*
ⲃ̄ⲣⲁ, pl. ⲃ̄ⲣⲏⲩⲉ v. ⲉⲃⲣⲁ *seed*
ⲃⲉⲣⲱ f. *whirlpool*
ⲃⲱⲱⲣⲉ, ⲃⲉⲉⲣⲉ-, ⲃⲟⲟⲣ⸗, ⲃⲟⲟⲣⲉ† *push, drive*
ⲃⲣ̄ⲃⲣ̄ [ⲃⲣ̄ⲃⲣⲉ] *boil*
ⲃⲣ̄ⲣⲉ *new, young*
ⲃⲁⲣⲱⲧ [ⲃⲉⲣⲱⲧ] m. *bronze*

[ⲃⲉⲣⲏ2] v. ⲙⲉⲣⲉ2 *spear*
ⲃⲏⲧ   m. *palm leaf*
   ⲃⲏⲧ   ⲥⲡⲓⲣ   f. *rib*
ⲃⲟⲧⲉ   f. *abomination, anathema*
   ⲝⲓⲃⲟⲧⲉ   *loathe, abhor*
ⲃⲱⲧⲉ, ϥⲱⲧⲉ, ⲃⲉⲧ-, ϥⲉⲧ-, ⲃⲏⲧ†, ϥⲏⲧ† *pollute, hate*
ⲃⲱⲱ, ⲃⲉⲱ-, ⲃⲟⲱ⸗, ⲃⲟϭ⸗ [ⲃⲱ⸗], ⲃⲏⲱ† *be loosened, strip, divest, release,*
   forsake
ⲃⲱⲉ *forgetfulness, sleep* v. ⲱⲃⲱ
ⲃⲁⲱⲟⲣ, pl. ⲃⲁⲱⲟⲟⲣ f. *fox*
ⲃⲁⲱⲟⲩⲣ   f. *saw*
ⲃⲁⲱⲟⲩⲱ   m. *rue*
ⲃⲁ2   m. *penis*
ⲃⲟⲩ2ⲉ [ϥⲟⲩ2ⲉ, ⲃⲁ2ⲟⲩ] m. *eyelid*
ⲃⲁ2ⲥⲉ   f. *heifer, calf*

ⲅ
called ⲅⲁⲙⲙⲁ   transliterated g

ⲅ̄   as number *three*
-ⲅ   for -ⲕ suffix pronoun 2nd person sing. masc.
ⲅ is rare except in words of Gk. derivation
Gk. γ is sometimes replaced by Coptic ⲕ

ⲇ
called ⲇⲁⲗⲇⲁ   transliterated d

ⲇ̄   as number *four*
ⲇ   is used only in words of Gk. derivation
ⲇ   sometimes interchanges with ⲧ [ⲓⲁⲗⲧⲁⲃⲁⲱⲑ for ⲓⲁⲗⲇⲁⲃⲁⲱⲑ]

ⲉ
called ⲉⲓ   transliterated e

ⲉ̄   as number *five*
[ⲉ   often interchanges with ⲁ]
[ⲉ   added after final ⲃ,ⲗ,ⲙ,ⲛ,ⲣ]
[ⲉ†, ⲉⲉ⸗, ⲉⲉⲧ⸗] v. ⲉⲓⲣⲉ
ⲉ- [ⲁ-], ⲉⲣⲟ⸗ [ⲁⲣⲁ⸗] *to, for, against, about, concerning, from, towards, until,*
   than
   ⲉⲧⲉⲣⲟ⸗ n. *debt*
   The paradigm for ⲉⲣⲟ⸗ and other presuffixal forms ending in ⲟ⸗ is this:
   ⲉⲣⲟⲓ̈ *to me*
   ⲉⲣⲟⲕ *to you* sing. masc.
   ⲉⲣⲟ *to you* sing. fem.
   ⲉⲣⲟϥ *to him*

ερος *to her*
ερον *to us*
ερωτⲛ̅ *to you* pl.
ερooγ *to them*
ε- [ⲁ-], ερo⸌ [ⲁⲣⲁ⸌] introduces direct object after verbs of cognition and perception
ε- [ⲁ-] with infinitive: coordinates a second verb *to* . . .
ε⸌, ερε- circumstantial converter *since, after, while, as, when, having*
ε⸌, ερε- [ε-] conjugation base II present
ε⸌ ⲛⲁ-, ερε- . . . ⲛⲁ- [ε- . . . ⲛⲁ-, ⲁ- . . . ⲛⲁ-] conjugation base II future
ε⸌ ε- conjugation base III future
-ε suffix pronoun 2nd person sing. fem. *you*, omitted after a vowel
ε⸌ ϣⲁⲛ- [ϣⲁ-], ερϣⲁⲛ- conjugation base conditional *if, when*
  ϩoⲧⲁⲛ ε⸌ ϣⲁⲛ- *whenever* (ὅταν)
  ε⸌ ⲧⲙ̅- (for ε⸌ ϣⲁⲛⲧⲙ̅-) negative conditional
εїε [ϩїε] *then*, introduces apodosis, interjection or interrogative
εⲱ, pl. εooγ v. εїⲱ *donkey*
εвн [n. *darkness*]
  ⲣ̅εвн *darken*
εвїⲱ m. *honey*
[εвo, εвⲱ] v. ⲙ̅пo *mute*
εвoⲗ *out* v. вoⲗ
εвιнⲛ m.f. *poor, wretched person*
εврⲁ, ⲃ̅рⲁ, pl. εврнγε, ⲃ̅рнγε m. *seed*
εврнбε, ⲃ̅врнбε [ϩїεврнⲝ, ϩвврнбε] f. *lightning*
εвoⲧ, pl. εвⲁⲧε, εвεⲧε m. *month* (of thirty days)
εκιвε, κιвε [бιвε] f. *breast, nipple*
[εκειⲁ†] v. κιⲧε *didrachm*
[ελⲱⲗ, εⲗⲁⲁⲧ†] *be impatient, anxious, worried*]
ελooⲗε [εⲗⲁⲁⲗε] m. *grape*
  ελεⲁϩⲙ̅ⲝ m. *sour grapes*
  вⲱ ⲛ̅ελooⲗε f. *grapevine*
  ⲙⲁ ⲛ̅ελooⲗε m. *vineyard*
[ελoγ] v. ⲁⲗoγ *child*
ελⲱ v. ⲗⲁⲱ *snare*
εⲙoγ, pl. εⲙooγε f. *cat*
εⲙⲛ̅ⲧ m. *west*
[εⲙⲛ̅ⲧε] v. ⲁⲙⲛ̅ⲧε *hell*
εⲙпⲁⲧε⸌ v. ⲙ̅пⲁⲧε⸌ conj. base *not yet*
εⲙнрε f. *flood, inundation*
εⲙιⲥε m. *dill*
εⲙⲁⲧε v. ⲙⲁⲧε *very much* and *only*
[εⲙⲁϣo *very much*]
[εⲙⲁϩⲧε] v. ⲁⲙⲁϩⲧε *prevail*
[εⲛ] v. ⲁⲛ negative particle
[εⲛⲁ⸌ in ⲣ̅εⲛⲁ⸌] *be pleasing to* v. ⲁⲛⲁї
εⲛε-, ⲛε- before question *whether*
εⲛε⸌, εⲛε- [ⲛε-] circumstantial of preterit *if . . . were, if . . . had*

ⲉⲛⲉ⸗, ⲉⲛⲉⲣⲉ- relative preterit
ⲉⲛⲉ⸗, ⲉⲛⲉⲣⲉ- II preterit
ⲉⲛⲉ- v. ⲱⲛⲉ *stone*
[ⲉⲛⲓ⸗] v. ⲉⲓⲛⲉ *bring*
ⲉⲛⲓⲙ *draw lots*
ⲉⲛⲧⲁ⸗, ⲛ̄ⲧⲁ⸗ [ⲉⲧⲁ⸗, ⲉⲛⲧⲁϩ⸗, ⲛ̄ⲧⲁϩ⸗], ⲉⲛⲧⲁ-, ⲛ̄ⲧⲁ- [ⲉⲛⲧⲁϩ-,
ⲛ̄ⲧⲁϩ-] conjugation base relative I perfect
[ⲉⲛⲁϣ] v. ⲁⲛⲁϣ *oath*
ⲉⲛⲉϩ [ⲁⲛⲏϩⲉ] m. *eternity, age, ever, eternal*
with negative *never*
ϣⲁⲉⲛⲉϩ *forever*
ⲉⲡⲏⲡ, ⲉⲡⲏⲫ name of 11th Egyptian month
ⲉⲡⲣⲁ *vain*
[ⲉⲣ-, ⲉⲣⲓ-] v. ⲉⲓⲣⲉ *make*
ⲉⲣⲉ- v. ⲉ⸗ circumstantial and conj. bases
ⲉⲣⲟ v. ⲣ̄ⲣⲟ *king*
ⲉⲣⲟ⸗ v. ⲉ- *to*
ⲉⲣⲛ̄-, ⲉⲣⲱ⸗ *to, upon, at* v. ⲣⲟ
[ⲉⲣⲡⲉ] v. ⲣ̄ⲡⲉ *temple*
ⲉⲣⲁⲧ⸗ *to* v. ⲣⲁⲧ⸗
ⲉⲣⲏⲧ, ⲣ̄ⲣⲏⲧ *vow, promise*; m. *promise*
ⲉⲣⲱⲧⲉ m. f. *milk*
ⲉⲣⲏⲩ [ⲉⲣⲏⲟⲩ] pl. *each other, one another*
takes possessive: ⲙ̄ⲛ̄ⲛⲉⲩⲉⲣⲏⲩ *with each other*
ⲉⲣϣⲁⲛ- v. ⲉ⸗ϣⲁⲛ- conj. base
ⲉⲣⲉϩ v. ϩⲁⲣⲉϩ *keep*
[ⲉⲥⲓⲉⲉⲓ] v. ⲁⲥⲁⲓ̈ *be light*
ⲉⲥⲏⲧ m. *ground, bottom*
ⲉⲡⲉⲥⲏⲧ *down, downwards*
ⲙ̄ⲡⲉⲥⲏⲧ *below*
ⲥⲁⲡⲉⲥⲏⲧ *below*
ϩⲁⲡⲉⲥⲏⲧ *under*
[ⲉⲥⲟⲧⲉ] v. ⲥⲟⲧⲉ *measure*
[ⲉⲥⲟⲩ] v. ⲁⲥⲟⲩ *price*
ⲉⲥⲟⲟⲩ [ⲉⲥⲁⲩ] m. *sheep*
ⲉⲧ-, ⲉⲧⲉ-, ⲉⲧⲉⲣⲉ-, ⲉⲧ⸗ relative converter *who, whom, which, that*
ⲡⲉⲧ- substantivized relative *the one who* or *which, he who, whoever*
ⲉⲧⲉⲡⲁⲓ̈ ⲡⲉ *that is, id est*
ⲉⲉⲧ† v. ⲱⲱ *conceive*
ⲉⲧⲉ- II tense with ⲙ̄ⲛ̄-, ⲙ̄ⲛ̄ⲧⲁ⸗
ⲉⲧⲃⲉ-, ⲉⲧⲃⲏⲏⲧ⸗ [ⲉⲧⲃⲏⲧ⸗] *because of, concerning, on account of, for the sake of*
ⲉⲧⲃⲉⲡⲁⲓ̈ *therefore*
ⲉⲧⲃⲉⲟⲩ *why?*
ⲉⲧⲃⲉⲝⲉ- *because*
ⲉⲧⲡⲱ *burden* v. ⲱⲧⲡ
ⲉⲧⲣⲉ⸗ v. ⲧⲣⲉ⸗ conj. base
ⲉⲧⲉⲣⲉ- v. ⲉⲧ- relative particle
ⲉⲧⲟⲟⲧ⸗ *to* v. ⲧⲱⲣⲉ

[ⲉⲩ] v. ⲟⲩ *what?*
ⲉⲟⲟⲩ [ⲉⲁⲩ] m. *glory*
ϯⲉⲟⲟⲩ ⲛⲁ⸗ *glorify*
ϫⲓⲉⲟⲟⲩ *be glorified*
ⲉⲩ- [ⲁⲩ-] (for ⲉⲟⲩ- with ⲟ eliding) preposition ⲉ- [ⲁ-] before indef. art. sing.
ⲉⲩⲱ, ⲉⲟⲩⲱ f. *pledge, deposit*
[ⲉⲟⲩⲁⲛ] v. ⲁⲩⲁⲛ *color*
ⲉϣ- v. ϣ- *be able to*
[ⲉϣ] v. ⲁϣ *what?*
ⲉϣⲁ⸗ v. ϣⲁ⸗ conj. base
ⲉϣⲱ f. *sow*
ϣⲉ, pl. ⲉϣⲁⲩ m. *pig*
ⲉϣⲱⲡⲉ [ⲉϣⲡⲉ, ⲉⲓϣⲡⲉ] *if* v. ϣⲱⲡⲉ
ⲉϣⲁⲣⲉ- v. ϣⲁ⸗ conj. base
ⲉϣⲱⲧ, pl. ⲉϣⲟⲧⲉ v. ϣⲱⲧ *trader*
ⲉϣϣⲉ v. ϣϣⲉ *be suitable*
ⲉϣϫⲉ- *if, as if, how!, indeed, then*
ⲉϣϫⲡⲉ means the same (ⲉϣϫⲉ plus ⲉϣⲱⲡⲉ)
ⲉϩⲉ, pl. ⲉϩⲟⲟⲩ m.f. *ox, cow*
ⲉϩⲉ, ϩⲉ, ⲁϩⲉ *yes, indeed*
ⲉϩⲏ, ⲉϩⲏⲧ⸗ v. ϩⲏ *front*
[ⲉϩⲟ, pl. ⲉϩⲱⲣ] v. ⲁϩⲟ *treasure*
ⲉϩⲟⲩⲉ-, ⲉϩⲟⲩⲉⲣⲟ⸗ *more than, rather than* v. ϩⲟⲩⲟ
ⲉϩⲟⲩⲛ ⲉ- *into* v. ϩⲟⲩⲛ
ⲉϩⲛⲉ-, ⲉϩⲛⲁ⸗ v. ϩⲛⲉ- *be willing*
ⲉϩⲣⲁï *upward, downward* v. ϩⲣⲁï
ⲉϩⲣⲛ̄-, ⲉϩⲣⲁ⸗ *to, among* v. ϩⲟ
ⲉϩⲧⲟ v. ϩⲧⲟ *horse*
ⲉϫⲏⲩ *ships* v. ϫⲟï
ⲉϫⲛ̄- [ⲁϫⲛ̄-], ⲉϫⲱ⸗ [ⲁϫⲱ⸗] *upon* v. ϫⲱ⸗
ⲉϫⲛ̄-, ⲉϫⲛ̄ⲧ⸗ v. ⲁϫⲛ̄- *without*
ⲉϭⲱϣ, pl. ⲉϭⲟⲟϣ m. *Ethiopian, Cushite*

ϛ

Greek letter digamma as number *six*

ⲍ

called ⲍⲏⲧⲁ transliterated *z*

ⲍ as number *seven*
ⲍ is rare except in words of Gk. derivation

H
called 2HTⲀ   transliterated ē̂

Ꞩ̄ as number *eight*
Hï, HЄI   m. *house*
   pⲘ̄N̄Hï   m.f. *member of household, relative, steward*
HN [HNЄ]   m. *ape*
Hⲡ† *be counted*† v. ⲱⲡ
HⲡЄ   *number* v. ⲱⲡ
HⲡⲤ v. ⲀⲡⲤ *number*
Hpⲡ, ЄРⲡ-, P̄ⲡ- m. *wine*
HⲤЄ *Isis*

Ɵ
called ƟHTⲀ   transliterated *th*

ꞩ̄ as number *nine*
Ɵ for Tꙴ, frequently the def. art. sing. fem. before a Coptic word with initial
   ꙴ or a Gk. word with rough breathing

ЄΙ, ῒ, Ι
called ΙⲱTⲀ   transliterated *ei, i*

T as number *ten*
ЄΙ is usually treated as a consonant (Middle Egyptian *y*)
ЄΙ [Ι] *come, be coming*†
   NHY† q.v., serves as the qualitative of ЄΙ
   imper. ⲀMOY q.v.
   ЄΙ ЄBOⲀ   *come out, leave*
   ЄΙ Є2OYN Є- *enter*
-ῒ [-ЄΙ] suffix pronoun 1st person sing. *me*
   -T following consonants but omitted after T
ЄΙⲀ m. *valley, ravine, cave*
ЄΙⲀ, ЄΙЄР-, ЄΙⲀT⸗ f. *eye* (only in compounds, cf. BⲀⲀ)
   Kⲱ 2ⲀЄΙⲀT⸗ *plan, intend*
   NⲀïⲀT⸗ [NЄЄΙЄT⸗] *blessed*
   TOYNЄΙⲀT⸗, TOYNOYЄΙⲀT⸗ *instruct*
ЄΙⲱ [ЄΙⲱЄ], ЄΙⲀ-, ЄΙⲀⲀ⸗, ЄΙH† *wash*
ЄΙⲱ, Єⲱ, ЄΙⲀ-, pl. ЄOOY m.f. *donkey*
ЄΙB, ЄΙЄΙB, pl. ЄΙЄBH m. *hoof, claw, sting, toenail*
ЄΙBЄ, OBЄ† *be thirsty;* m. *thirst*
ЄΙЄBT [ЄΙB̄TЄ, ⲀЄΙB̄TЄ] m. *east*
ЄΙⲀⲀ, ïⲀⲀ [ЄΙЄⲀ] f. *mirror*
ЄΙOYⲀ m.f. *deer*
ЄΙOM m. *wine vat*
ЄΙMЄ [M̄MЄ, ΙMЄ] *know, understand;* [m. *knowledge*]
   MN̄TⲀTЄΙMЄ f. *ignorance*

ⲈⲒⲚⲈ [ⲒⲚⲈ], Ⲛ̄-, Ⲛ̄ⲦⲈ̄ [ⲈⲚⲒⲈ̄] *bring, carry*
    imper. ⲀⲚⲈⲒⲚⲈ, ⲀⲚⲒⲈ̄ [ⲈⲚⲒⲈ̄]
ⲈⲒⲚⲈ [ⲒⲚⲈ] (Ⲛ̄-, Ⲙ̄ⲘⲞⲈ̄) *resemble, be like;* m. *likeness, image*
ⲈⲒⲚⲈ m. *chain*
ⲈⲒⲞⲠⲈ, ⲈⲒⲈⲠ- f. *craft, trade, occupation*
    ⲈⲒⲈⲠϢⲰⲦ *engage in business, trade;* m. *merchandise*
ⲈⲒⲞⲞⲢ m. *irrigation canal*
    ⲪⲒⲞⲞⲢ *ferry, ford*
    ⲀⲦⲬⲒⲞⲞⲢ *inaccessible*
    ⲈⲒⲈⲢⲞ, Ⲓ̈ⲈⲢⲞ, pl. Ⲓ̈ⲈⲢⲰⲞⲨ m. *river, Nile* (-Ⲟ)
ⲈⲒⲢⲈ, Ⲣ̄- [ⲈⲢ-], ⲀⲀⲈ̄ [ⲀⲈ̄, ⲈⲈⲈ̄, ⲈⲈⲦⲈ̄], ⲞⲦ [ⲞⲈⲒ†, Ⲉ†] *make, do, perform,*
    become, produce, spend(time), be†
    imper. ⲀⲢⲒⲢⲈ, ⲀⲢⲒ- [ⲈⲢⲒ-], ⲀⲢⲒⲈ̄
    Ⲣ̄- is used with many nouns to create compound verbs, cf. Ⲣ̄ⲚⲞⲂⲈ etc.
    [Ⲣ̄- is used as an auxiliary with Gk. verbs]
ⲈⲒⲰⲢⲘ̄, ⲈⲒⲞⲢⲘ̄† [ⲈⲒⲀⲢⲘ̄†] *stare, gaze, be astonished,* [*grant, consent*]
ⲈⲒⲰⲢⲠ̄ *see, perceive;* m. *sight*
ⲈⲒⲤ-, ⲈⲒⲤϨⲎⲎⲦⲈ, ⲈⲒⲤϨⲎⲎⲠⲈ *behold!, indeed!*
[ⲒⲰⲤ, ⲒⲎⲤ† *hasten, hurry;* m. *speed*]
ⲈⲒⲀⲦⲈ̄ v. ⲈⲒⲀ *eye*
ⲈⲒⲰⲦ, Ⲓ̈ⲰⲦ, pl. ⲈⲒⲞⲦⲈ [ⲈⲒⲀⲦⲈ] m. *father,* pl. *parents*
ⲈⲒⲰⲦ m. *barley*
ⲈⲒⲰⲦⲈ f. *dew*
ⲈⲒⲦⲚ̄, ⲒⲦⲚ̄ m. *ground, earth, dirt*
    ⲈⲠⲒⲦⲚ̄ *down*
    ⲤⲀⲘ̄ⲠⲒⲦⲚ̄ m. *bottom, below*
ⲈⲒⲀⲀⲨ m. *linen*
ⲈⲒϢⲈ, ⲀϢⲦ-, ⲈϢⲦ-, ⲀϢⲦⲈ̄, ⲀϢⲈ† [ⲞϢⲈ†] *hang, suspend, depend, crucify*
[ⲈⲒϢⲠⲈ] *if* v. ϢⲰⲠⲈ
ⲈⲒϤⲦ m. *nail* v. ⲰϤⲦ
ⲈⲒⲰϨⲈ, ⲈⲒⲈϨ, pl. ⲈⲒⲀϨⲞⲨ m. *field*
    ⲤⲦⲈⲒⲰϨⲈ, ⲤⲦⲰϨⲈ f. *acre*

Ⲕ

called ⲕⲀⲠⲠⲀ transliterated *k*

Ⲕ̄ as number *twenty*
ⲕ sometimes interchanges with ϭ
ⲕ sometimes replaces Gk. ⲅ
ⲕ- personal pronoun 2nd person sing. masc. *you*
-ⲕ suffix pronoun 2nd person sing. masc. *you*
ⲕⲈ, ϬⲈ, pl. ⲕⲞⲞⲨⲈ [ⲕⲀⲨⲈ], ⲕⲈⲕⲞⲞⲨⲈ [ⲕⲈⲕⲀⲨⲈ, ⲕⲈⲕⲈⲨⲈ] m.f. *another, other*
    ⲕⲈ- [ϬⲈ-] *other, even*
    Ⲛ̄ⲕⲈⲤⲞⲠ *again*
    ⲕⲈⲞⲨⲀ [ⲕⲈⲨⲈ] *another*
    ⲠⲕⲈ- (with def. art.) may mean *also, even*
    ⲕⲈⲦ, f. ⲕⲈⲦⲈ *another, other*
ⲕⲞⲨⲒ̈ [ⲕⲞⲨⲈⲒ], ⲕⲞⲨ- m.f. *young person, little one*

ⲕⲟⲩⲓ ⲛ̄- *small, few*

ⲕⲉⲕⲟⲩⲓ *yet a little while*

ⲕⲟⲩⲓ ⲕⲟⲩⲓ *little by little*

ⲕⲱ [ⲕⲱⲉ], ⲕⲁ- [ⲕⲉ-], ⲕⲁⲁ⸗ [ⲕⲟⲟ⸗], ⲕⲏⲧ [ⲕⲁⲁⲧⲧ] *place, put, set, permit, abandon, lie†, be†*

ⲕⲱ ⲉⲃⲟⲗ *forgive, release, dismiss*

ⲕⲱ ⲛ̄ⲥⲁ, ⲛ̄ⲥⲱ⸗ *leave behind, renounce*

ⲕⲱ ⲛ̄ⲧⲛ̄-, ⲛ̄ⲧⲟⲟⲧ⸗ *entrust to*

ⲕⲏ ⲉϩⲣⲁⲓ *be laid down, exist*

[ⲕⲁⲁⲥ f. *foundation*]

ⲕⲱⲃ, ⲕⲃ̄-, ⲕⲟⲃ⸗, ⲕⲏⲃⲧ *be double, fold; m. return, repetition*

ϣⲙ̄ⲧⲕⲱⲃ *threefold* (ϣⲟⲙⲛ̄ⲧ)

ⲕⲓⲃⲉ v. ⲉⲕⲓⲃⲉ *breast*

ⲕⲱⲱⲃⲉ, ⲕⲱⲱϭⲉ, ⲕⲉⲉⲃⲉ-, ⲕⲉϭⲉ-, ⲕⲁⲁⲃⲉ-, ⲕⲟⲟⲃⲉ⸗ *compel, force, seize*

ⲕⲃⲁ m. *compulsion*

ⲕⲃⲟ, ⲕⲃⲁ, ⲕⲃⲉ-, ⲕⲏⲃⲧ *be cool, cool; m. coolness*

ⲕⲃⲁ m. *revenge*

ⲕⲱⲕ, ⲕⲉⲕ-, ⲕⲟⲕ⸗, ⲕⲁⲕ⸗, ⲕⲁⲁⲕ⸗, ⲕⲏⲕⲧ [ⲕⲁⲕⲧ] *peel, strip, divest*

ⲕⲱⲕ ⲁϩⲏⲩ, ⲕⲱⲕ ⲉϩⲏⲩ *strip naked*

also written ⲕⲱ, ⲕⲁⲁ⸗ ⲕⲁϩⲏⲩ

ⲕⲁⲕⲉ [ⲕⲉⲕⲉ, ⲕⲉⲕⲉⲓ] m. *darkness*

ⲕⲉⲗⲉⲃⲓⲛ m. *axe, pickaxe*

ⲕⲁⲗⲉⲗⲉ, ⲕⲉⲗⲉⲉⲗⲉ f. *board, stick*

ⲕⲗ̄ⲗⲉ f. *bolt, knee, joint*

ⲕⲉⲗⲉⲛⲕⲉϩ m. *elbow*

ⲕⲉⲗⲱⲗ m. *pitcher, bucket*

ⲕⲗⲟⲟⲗⲉ f. *cloud*

[ⲕⲱⲗⲉⲙ *hurry*]

ⲕⲗⲟⲙ [ⲕⲗⲁⲙ], pl. ⲕⲗⲟⲟⲙ m. *crown, wreath*

ⲕⲱⲗⲡ *steal, rob*

ⲕⲗⲯ in ⲧⲕⲗⲯ *hit, punch*

ⲕⲗⲁϥⲧ f. *hood, cowl*

ⲕⲱⲗϩ, ⲕⲟⲗϩ *strike, knock*

ⲕⲁⲗⲁϩⲏ f. *womb*

ⲕⲱⲗⲝ, ϭⲱⲗⲝ, ⲕⲁⲝ-, ⲕⲟⲗⲝ⸗, ⲕⲟⲗⲝⲧ, ϭⲟⲗⲝⲧ *bend*

ⲕⲗ̄ⲝⲉ f. *corner, angle*

ⲕⲓⲙ [ⲕⲉⲓⲙ], ⲕⲉⲙⲧ-, ⲕⲉⲙⲧ⸗ *move, be moved; m. motion*

ⲁⲧⲕⲓⲙ *unshakable, immovable, unwavering*

ⲕⲙ̄ⲧⲟ m. *earthquake*

ⲕⲙⲟⲙ, ⲕⲏⲙⲧ *become black, be black†*

ⲕⲁⲙⲉ m.f. *black thing* or *person, black*

ⲕⲏⲙⲉ *Egypt*

ⲧⲙⲛ̄ⲧⲣⲙ̄ⲛ̄ⲕⲏⲙⲉ *the Coptic language*

ⲕⲙⲏⲙⲉ n. *darkness*

ⲕⲱⲙϣ, ⲕⲙ̄ϣ-, ⲕⲟⲙϣ⸗ *sneer, mock; m. mockery*

ⲕⲟⲩⲛ⸗, ⲕⲟⲩⲟⲩⲛ⸗, ⲕⲟⲩⲛⲧ⸗ n. *bosom of, lap of, genitals of*

ⲕⲛ̄ⲛⲉ *be fat, sweet; m. fatness, sweetness*

ⲕⲱⲛⲥ, ⲕⲉⲛⲥ-, ⲕⲟⲛⲥ⸗, ⲕⲟⲛⲥⲧ *pierce, slay*

ⲕⲛ̄ⲧⲉ m. *fig*

ΚΑΠ m. *receptacle, vessel*
ΚⲰΠ, ΚΗΠⲦ *hide*
ΚΗΠⲈ f. *vault, roof, cellar*
[ΚΗΠⲈ] v. ϬΗΠⲈ *cloud*
ΚΟΥΠⲢ m. *henna, flower*
ΚΟΥⲢ n. *deaf person, hearing impaired person*
ΚⲢΟ, pl. ΚⲢⲰΟΥ m. *shore, bank, farther side*
ΚⲀⲢⲰ⸗, ΚⲀⲢⲀⲈΙⲦⲦ *be silent* v. ⲢΟ
ΚⲰⲰⲢⲈ, ΚⲈⲈⲢⲈ-, ΚΟΟⲢⲈ⸗ *cut down, be cut down*
ΚⲢⲰⲘ m. *fire*
ΚⲢⲘ̄ⲢⲘ̄ *murmur;* m. *muttering, complaint*
ΚⲢΟⲘⲢⲘ̄, ΚⲢⲘ̄ⲢⲰⲘⲦ *be dark*
    ΚⲢⲘ̄ⲦⲤ m. *smoke, mist, darkness*
ΚⲢ̄ⲘⲈⲤ m.f. *ash, dust*
ΚⲢΟΥⲢ m. *frog*
ΚⲰⲢⲰ̣ (Ⲉ-) *beg, request, persuade;* m. *persuasion*
ΚⲢΟϤ m. *deceitfulness, cunning, falsehood, cheater*
ΚⲀⲤ, ΚⲈⲈⲤ, ΚΗⲤ, pl. ΚⲀⲀⲤ m. *bone*
ΚⲰⲰⲤ, ΚΟΟⲤ⸗, ΚΗⲤⲦ *prepare for burial, bury;* m. *corpse, burial*
    ΚⲀΙⲤⲈ f. *burial, shroud*
ΚⲀⲤΚⲤ *whisper;* m. *gossip*
ΚΟⲤΚⲤ, ΚⲈⲤΚⲰⲤ⸗ (ⲈⲂΟⲖ) *bend, stretch out*
ϨΟΥⲢ m. *ring*
ΚⲈⲦ, ΚⲈⲦⲈ v. ΚⲈ *another*
ΚⲰⲦ, ΚⲈⲦ-, ΚΟⲦ⸗, ΚΗⲦⲦ *build, edify, build up;* m. *building, edification*
[ΚⲰⲦ] v. ΚⲰϨⲦ *fire*
ΚⲀⲦΟ f. *boat*
ΚΙⲦⲈ [pl. ⲈΚⲈΙⲀⲦ] f. *didrachm, silver coin*
ΚⲰⲦⲈ, ΚⲈⲦ-, ΚΟⲦ⸗ [ΚⲀⲦ⸗, ΚⲰⲦ⸗], ΚΗⲦⲦ *turn, go around, wander, seek*
    ΚⲰⲦⲈ Ⲉ- *surround, seek*
    ΚⲰⲦⲈ Ⲙ̄ΜΟ⸗, ΚΟⲦ⸗ *turn oneself, return, repeat, resume*
    ΚⲰⲦⲈ Ⲛ̄ΚⲀ-, Ⲛ̄ΚⲰ⸗ *seek, look for*
    ΚⲰⲦⲈ m. *circuit, surroundings*
    Ⲙ̄ΠΚⲰⲦⲈ *around*
    ΚΟⲦ m. *turn, visit*
    ΚΟⲦ, ΚⲀⲦ m. *wheel, basket*
    ΚΟⲦⲤ f. *crookedness, trick*
ΚⲦΟ v. [ⲦΚⲀⲦΟ] *turn*
ΚⲰⲦϤ, ΚⲈⲦϤ-, ΚΟⲦϤ⸗, [ΚⲀⲦϤ⸗] ΚΟⲦϤⲦ *gather*
ΚΟΟΥ m. *length of time*
ΚⲀⲰ̣ m. *reed, pen*
ΚⲀϨ m. *earth, soil, land*
ΚΟⲈΙϨ, ΚⲀΪϨ [ΚⲀⲈΙϨⲈ] m. *sheath, cover*
ΚΟΟϨ, ΚⲰϨ m. *corner, point, piece*
ΚⲰϨ, ΚΗϨⲦ (Ⲉ-) *envy, be jealous;* m. *envy*
ΚⲰϨ, ΚⲈϨ-, ΚⲀϨ⸗, ΚΗϨⲦ *make level, smooth, tame*
ΚΟΙⲀϨΚ, ΧΟΙⲀϨΚ *name of 4th Egyptian month*
ΚⲀϨΚϨ, ΚⲈϨΚⲰϨ⸗, ΚⲈϨΚⲰϨⲦ *carve out, smooth*
ΚⲰϨⲦ [ΚⲰⲦ] m. *fire*

ⲕⲁϩⲏⲩ in ⲕⲱ,ⲕⲁⲁ⸗ ⲕⲁϩⲏⲩ v. ⲕⲱⲕ

ⲗ
called ⲗⲁⲩⲇⲁ transliterated *l*

ⲗ̄ as number *thirty*
[ⲗ̄- can stand for ⲛ̄-]
ⲗⲁ̀ m. *envy, slander*
   ϩⲓⲗⲁ *slander* (ϩⲓⲟⲩⲉ)
ⲗⲟ [ⲗⲱ,ⲗⲟⲧ⸗], imper. ⲁⲗⲟ⸗ *stop, quit, be healed*
ⲗⲓⲃⲉ,ⲗⲉⲃⲧ⸗,ⲗⲟⲃⲉᵗ [ⲗⲁⲃⲉᵗ] *be mad;* m. *madness*
ⲗⲱⲃϣ,ⲗⲟⲃϣᵗ *be hot, glow;* m. *heat*
ⲗⲱⲃϣ m. *crown*
ⲗⲱⲕ,ⲗⲏⲕᵗ *be soft, fresh*
ⲗⲁⲕϻ̄ f. *piece*
ⲗⲱⲕⲥ *bite, stick*
ⲗ̄ⲕϣⲁ *sneer* v. ϣⲗⲁⲕ
ⲗⲉⲗⲟⲩ [ⲗⲓⲗⲟⲩ] m.f. *child, boy, girl*
ⲗⲟⲩⲗⲁⲓ̈ m. *shout*
ⲗ̄ⲗⲏⲃ m. *ridicule*
ⲗⲱⲱⲙⲉ,ⲗⲱⲱⲙ,ⲗⲟⲟⲙⲉᵗ,ⲗⲁⲁⲙⲉᵗ,ⲗⲁⲁⲙᵗ *wither, fade, be dirty*ᵗ; m. *dirt*
ⲗⲱⲙⲥ,ⲗⲟⲙⲥᵗ *be dirty, foul, stink*
ⲗⲁⲥ [ⲗⲉⲥ] m. *tongue, language*
ⲗⲱⲱⲥ *be bruised, crushed*
ⲗⲁⲁⲩ,ⲗⲁⲁⲩⲉ,ⲗⲁⲩⲉ n. *anyone, something* (with positive), *no one, nothing*
   (with negative)
ⲗⲟⲟⲩ,ⲗⲁⲩ m. *curl, fringe, bunch*
ⲗⲁⲩⲟ m.f. *sail*
ⲗⲟϥⲗϥ,ⲗⲉϥⲗⲟϥⲧᵗ *rot, perish, destroy*
   ⲗⲉϥⲗⲓϥⲉ f. *scrap, crumb*
ⲗⲟⲓ̈ϩⲉ [ⲗⲁⲉⲓϩⲉ] m.f. *mud, filth*
ⲗ̄ϩⲱⲃ m. *steam, smoke*
ⲗⲁϩⲗⲉϩ [ⲗⲉϩⲗϩ,ⲗⲁϩⲗ̄] m. *height, pride*
ⲗ̄ϩⲏⲙ,ⲉⲗⲁϩⲏⲙ *roar*
[ⲗⲁϩⲙⲉⲛ] v. ϩ̄ⲣ̄ⲙⲁⲛ *pomegranate*
ⲗⲟⲭⲗⲭ,ⲗⲟⲃⲗⲉⲭ,ⲗⲉⲭⲗⲱⲭᵗ *be ill, sick;* [ⲗⲁⲭⲗⲉⲭ] m. *sickness*
ⲗⲱⲱϩ,ⲗⲉⲭϩ-,ⲗⲟⲭϩ⸗,ⲗⲟⲭϩᵗ *crush, be crushed, erase, lick, be difficult*ᵗ;
   m. *oppression*
ⲗⲟϭ,ⲗⲁϭ in ϩ̄ⲣ̄ⲗⲟϭ *be impudent, persistent*
[ⲗⲁϭⲉ,ⲗⲁϭ⸗ *cease, recover, cure*]
ⲗⲟⲓ̈ϭⲉ [ⲗⲁⲉⲓϭⲉ] f. *cause, excuse*

ϻ
called ⲙⲏ transliterated *m*

ϻ as number *forty*
ϻ- for ⲛ̄- before [ⲃ],ⲙ,ⲡ,ⲯ,ⲫ

ма m. *place*
  євоλ 2ѝпеїма *from here, away*
  епеїма *to this place, here*
  епма ѝ- *in place of, instead of*
  єүма *together* (є-оү)
  [(2)ѝнеєіма *here*]
ма-, мнеі⸗, ма† imper. of † and t-causative vbs.
[маєін f. *size, importance, age, stature*]
ме [меєіє, маєіє], мере- [ѝрре-], меріт⸗ [ѝрріт⸗], p.c. маї- *love, like;*
  m. *love*
  меріт [ѝѝріт], pl. мерате [ѝрре†] *beloved*
ме, меє, мне [міє] f. *truth, justice*
  наме [мамне, маміє] *truly, really*
ме⸗ [ма⸗], мере- [маре-] conjugation base negative habitual
мн f. *urine*
  мн ѝмооү f. *urine*
  мн оєік [мамоү ѝоєік] f. *feces*
міо⸗ *be well, thanks, hail!, hello!*
мо, pl. ѝмнеітѝ *take!*
моү, мооүт† [маүт†, маоүт†] *die, be dead†; m. death*
  намоү *is dying* (на future auxiliary)
моүе f. *island*
моүї, моүеі m.f. *lion*
мааb, f. мааbе, маb- *thirty*
мокмек [макмек], мекмоүк⸗ [моүкмоүк⸗] *ponder, meditate, consider;*
  m. *thought*
мак2 m. *neck*
моүк2, мек2-, мок2⸗ *afflict, oppress*
ѝка2, мок2† *be painful, difficult;* pl. ѝкоо2 m. *pain, difficulty, grief*
  хіѝка2 *suffer*
  ѝка2 ѝ2нт m. *pain, grief*
  мок2с f. *pain, grief*
мелωт f. *ceiling*
ѝλа2, pl. ѝλоо2 m. *battle, fight*
моүλ2, моλ2⸗, моλ2† *salt, be salty*
  мā2 n. *salt*
моүλ2 m. *wax*
моүλ2, моλ2⸗ [мαλ2⸗], моλ2† *be bound to, attached to, fasten, involve*
[мамне, маміє] *truly* v. ме *truth*
[ѝме] v. єіме *know*
ѝмо⸗ v. ѝ-
ѝмѝ-, мѝ- *there is not, are not* (negative existential predicate, opposite оүѝ-)
  мѝте-, мѝта⸗, мѝте⸗, мѝт⸗ *have not, has not*
  ѝмон [ѝман] *no, if not*
  хѝммон *or not, rather, or*
ѝмін ѝмо⸗ [ѝма⸗] *self, own*
ѝмон [еммон, ѝман] *truly, for*
мѝ- [мѝѝ- before оү], нѝма⸗ [нѝме⸗] *with, and*
  мѝѝса-, мѝѝсω⸗ *after*

ⲘⲚ̄Ⲛ̄ⲤⲀⲦⲢⲈ⸗ *after*
[ⲘⲚ̄-] v. Ⲙ̄ⲠⲢ̄- negative imper.
ⲘⲀⲈⲓⲚ   m. *sign, mark, wonder*
    †ⲘⲀⲈⲓⲚ *signify, indicate*
ⲘⲞⲨⲚ, ⲘⲎⲚⁿ (ⲈⲂⲞⲗ) *remain, continue;* m. *perseverance*
ⲘⲎⲚⲈ in Ⲙ̄ⲘⲎⲚⲈ *daily, every day*
ⲘⲓⲚⲈ f. *type, kind, nature, quality, fashion, sort*
ⲘⲞⲞⲚⲈ [ⲘⲞⲚⲈ, ⲘⲀⲚⲈ] *pasture, feed*
    ⲘⲀⲚⲈ, ⲘⲀⲚ- m. *herdsman, -herd*
    ⲘⲞⲞⲚⲈ, ⲘⲈⲚⲈ-, ⲘⲀⲚⲈ-, ⲘⲀⲚⲞⲨ-, ⲘⲀⲚⲞⲞⲨⲦⁿ *come to land, come into port*
ⲘⲞⲞⲚⲈ f. *nurse*
ⲘⲞⲨⲚⲔ, ⲘⲞⲨⲚⲄ [ⲘⲞⲨⲞⲨⲄ] m. *make, form;* m. *form, formation*
    [ⲘⲞⲨⲚⲔ Ⲛ̄ⲈⲞ m. *countenance*]
    ⲘⲞⲨⲚⲄ Ⲛ̄Ϭⲓⲝ m. *hand-made thing*
[ⲘⲞⲨⲚⲔ, ⲘⲞⲨⲚⲄ, ⲘⲞⲚⲔ⸗ *cease, perish, destroy*]
ⲘⲚ̄Ⲛ̄ⲤⲀ-, ⲘⲚ̄Ⲛ̄ⲤⲰ⸗ *after* v. ⲤⲀ
ⲘⲚ̄Ⲧ- forms abstract nouns fem. *-ness, -hood*
ⲘⲚ̄Ⲧ- v. ⲘⲎⲦ *ten*
Ⲙ̄ⲚⲞⲨⲦ m. *doorman, gatekeeper*
ⲘⲚ̄ⲦⲢⲈ, pl. ⲘⲚ̄ⲦⲢⲈⲈⲨ [ⲘⲚ̄ⲦⲢⲈⲞⲨ] m. *witness*
    Ⲣ̄ⲘⲚ̄ⲦⲢⲈ *testify*
    ⲘⲚ̄ⲦⲘⲚ̄ⲦⲢⲈ f. *testimony*
Ⲙ̄Ⲡ⸗, Ⲙ̄ⲠⲈ- conjugation base negative I perfect
    Ⲙ̄ⲠⲈ *no, if not,* or *not*
Ⲙ̄ⲠⲞ, ⲈⲘⲠⲞ [ⲈⲂⲞ, ⲈⲂⲰ] n. *mute, speechless person*
Ⲙ̄ⲠⲢ̄- [ⲘⲚ̄-], Ⲙ̄ⲠⲰⲣ negative imper. *do not*
    Ⲙ̄ⲠⲢ̄ⲦⲢⲈ⸗ [ⲘⲚ̄ⲦⲢⲈ⸗] negative causative imper.
Ⲙ̄ⲠⲀⲦⲈ⸗, Ⲙ̄ⲠⲀⲦⲈ- conjugation base *not yet*
    ⲈⲘⲠⲀⲦⲈ⸗ (with circumstantial) *before* (the spellings of Ⲙ̄ⲠⲀⲦⲈ⸗ and
    ⲈⲘⲠⲀⲦⲈ⸗ are often confused.)
Ⲙ̄Ⲡϣⲁ *be worthy, deserve;* m. *worth, fate*
    Ⲣ̄Ⲙ̄Ⲡϣⲁ *become worthy, be worthy*
[Ⲙ̄Ⲡϣⲁ *very much*]
ⲘⲞⲨⲣ, ⲘⲞⲣ⸗ [ⲘⲀⲣ⸗], ⲘⲎⲣⁿ, p.c. ⲘⲀⲣ-, ⲘⲈⲣ- *bind, tie, be tied*ⁿ, *be a prisoner*ⁿ
    Ⲙ̄ⲢⲢⲈ f. *chain, bond, fetter*
ⲘⲀⲢⲈ⸗, ⲘⲀⲢⲈ- causative imperative *let*
    absolute ⲘⲀⲢⲞⲚ *let's go*
ⲘⲈⲢⲈ- [Ⲙ̄ⲢⲢⲈ-], ⲘⲈⲢⲓⲦ⸗ [Ⲙ̄ⲢⲢⲓⲦ⸗] v. ⲘⲈ *love*
ⲘⲈⲢⲈ- [ⲘⲀⲢⲈ-] v. ⲘⲈ⸗ conj. base neg. habitual
ⲘⲈⲈⲢⲈ f. *noon, midday*
Ⲙ̄ⲢⲰ f. *harbor*
Ⲙ̄Ⲣⲓ̄Ⲥ m. *new wine*
ⲘⲈⲢⲓⲦ, pl. ⲘⲈⲢⲀⲦⲈ *beloved* v. ⲘⲈ *love*
ⲘⲞⲢⲦ f. *beard*
ⲘⲈⲢⲈⲈ [ⲂⲈⲢⲎⲈ] m. *spear*
ⲘⲞⲨⲤ m. *strap, thong*
ⲘⲓⲤⲈ, ⲘⲈⲤ-, ⲘⲀⲤⲦ⸗, ⲘⲈⲤⲦ⸗, ⲘⲞⲤⲈⁿ, p.c. ⲘⲀⲤ- *give birth, bear;* m. *child,*
    generation
    ϢⲢ̄ⲠⲘⲓⲤⲈ, ϢⲀⲘⲓⲤⲈ m. *first born child*

ϩⲟⲟⲩ ⲙ̄ⲙⲓⲥⲉ, ϩⲟⲩⲙⲓⲥⲉ   m. *birthday*
ⲙⲁⲥ   m. *young* (animal)
ⲙⲁⲥⲉ   m. *calf, kid, young animal*
ⲙⲏⲥⲉ   f. *usury, interest*
ⲙⲏⲥⲟⲣⲏ   name of 12th Egyptian month (birth of Ra)
ⲙⲉⲥⲓⲱ   f. *midwife, nurse*
ⲙⲟⲥⲧⲉ [ⲙⲁⲥⲧⲉ], ⲙⲉⲥⲧⲉ-, ⲙⲉⲥⲧⲱⲋ, p.c. ⲙⲁⲥⲧ- *hate*; m. *hatred*
  ⲙⲉⲥⲧⲉ, f. ⲙⲉⲥⲧⲏ n. *hated person*
ⲙⲉⲥⲉⲑⲏⲧ, ⲙⲉⲥⲧⲛ̄ϩⲏⲧ f. *chest, breast*
ⲙⲏⲧ, f. ⲙⲏⲧⲉ, ⲙⲛ̄ⲧ- *ten*
ⲙⲟⲉⲓⲧ [ⲙⲁⲉⲓⲧ] m. *road, path*
  ϫⲓⲙⲟⲉⲓⲧ (ϩⲏⲧⲋ) *lead, guide*
  ϫⲁⲩⲙⲟⲉⲓⲧ m. *leader, guide* (ϫⲓ)
ⲙⲟⲩⲧ   m. *sinew, nerve*
  ⲙⲟⲧⲉ   m. *neck, shoulders*
ⲙⲁⲧⲉ [ⲙⲉⲧⲉ, ⲙⲉⲉⲧⲉ], ⲙⲁⲧⲱⲟⲩᵗ [ⲙ̄ⲧⲱⲟⲩᵗ] *reach, attain, meet, enjoy*
  †ⲙⲁⲧⲉ *approve, consent; assent*
ⲙⲁⲧⲉ [ⲙⲉⲧⲉ] in ⲉⲙⲁⲧⲉ, ⲙ̄ⲙⲁⲧⲉ *very much, really*
ⲙⲁⲧⲉ in ⲙ̄ⲙⲁⲧⲉ, ⲉⲙⲁⲧⲉ *only, merely*
ⲙⲁⲧⲟⲓ̈ [ⲙⲁⲧⲁⲉⲓ] m. *soldier*
  ⲙⲛ̄ⲧⲙⲁⲧⲟⲓ̈ f. *army, campaign*
ⲙⲏⲧⲉ   f. *midst, middle*
ⲙⲟⲩⲧⲉ (ⲉ-) *call, summon, invoke*; m. *incantation*
ⲙ̄ⲧⲟ   m. *presence*
  ⲙ̄ⲡⲙ̄ⲧⲟ ⲉⲃⲟⲗ ⲛ̄- *before, in front of*
ⲙ̄ⲧⲱ   f. *depth*
ⲙ̄ⲧⲟⲛ [ⲙ̄ⲧⲁⲛ], ⲙⲟⲧⲛ̄ᵗ *be at rest, easy*ᵗ*, restful*ᵗ; m. *rest, ease, relief, repose*
  ⲙ̄ⲧⲟⲛ ⲙ̄ⲙⲟⲋ *rest oneself, die*(reflexive)
  ⲙⲟⲧⲛⲉⲥ f. *ease, satisfaction*
ⲙⲟⲩⲧⲛ̄, ⲙⲉⲧⲛ-, ⲙⲟⲧⲛⲋ *rest, set, agree*
ⲙⲁⲧⲟⲩ   f. *poison*
ⲙⲁⲩ in ⲙ̄ⲙⲁⲩ [ⲙ̄ⲙⲉⲩ] *there*
  (often follows ⲟⲩⲛⲧⲁⲋ and ⲙⲛ̄ⲧⲁⲋ and is untranslated)
  ⲉⲧⲙ̄ⲙⲁⲩ *that*
  ⲉⲙⲁⲩ *to that place, there*
ⲙⲁⲁⲩ, ⲙⲁⲩ [ⲙⲉⲉⲩ] f. *mother*
ⲙⲟⲟⲩ [ⲙⲁⲩ, ⲙⲁⲟⲩ], ⲙⲟⲩ-, pl. ⲙⲟⲩⲉⲓⲏ, ⲙⲟⲩⲉⲓⲟⲟⲩⲉ m. *water*
  ⲙⲉϩⲙⲟⲟⲩ *draw water* (ⲙⲟⲩϩ)
  ⲙⲟⲩⲙⲉ f. *spring, fountain*
ⲙⲁⲩⲁⲁⲋ, ⲙⲁⲩⲁⲁⲧⲋ *alone* v. ⲟⲩⲱⲧ
ⲙⲉⲉⲩⲉ, ⲙⲉⲩⲉ [ⲙⲉⲟⲩⲉ, ⲙⲉⲩⲟⲩⲉ] (ⲉ-) *think, believe*; m. *thought, mind*
  ⲣ̄ⲡⲙⲉⲉⲩⲉ ⲛ̄- *remember*
  †ⲙⲉⲉⲩⲉ *suggest, hint, remind*
ⲙⲟⲟⲩⲧᵗ *be dead*ᵗ v. ⲙⲟⲩ
ⲙⲟⲩⲟⲩⲧ, ⲙⲟⲩⲧ-, ⲙⲉⲩⲧ-, ⲙⲟⲟⲩⲧⲋ *kill*
ⲙⲁϣⲉ   f. *balance*
ⲙⲉϣⲉ, ⲙⲉϣⲁⲋ *does not know*
  ⲙⲉϣⲉ ⲛⲓⲙ *so-and-so*
  ⲙⲉϣⲁⲕ [ⲙⲉϣⲉⲕⲉ] *perhaps*

ⲘⲎⲎϢⲈ [ⲘⲎϢⲈ] m. *multitude, crowd*
    ⲘⲎⲎϢⲈ Ⲛ̄- *many*
ⲘⲒϢⲈ *fight, attack;* m. *fight, struggle, battle*
ⲘⲞⲞϢⲈ [ⲘⲀⲀⲌⲈ, ⲘⲀⲌⲈ] *walk, go, travel, wander;* m. *journey*
ⲘϢⲒⲢ name of 6th Egyptian month
ⲘⲞⲨϢⲦ, ⲘⲈϢⲦ-, ⲘⲞϢⲦⲋ *test, examine, reflect, consider*
    ⲘⲞϢⲦⲈ, ⲘⲞⲞϢⲈ pl. *environs, district*
ⲘⲈϢϢⲈ, ⲘϢϢⲈ *be inappropriate, not fitting* (neg. of ϢϢⲈ)
ⲘⲀⲌ m. *nest*
ⲘⲞⲨⲌ, ⲘⲈⲌ- [ⲘⲀⲌ-], ⲘⲀⲌⲋ, ⲘⲈⲌⲧ, ⲘⲎⲌⲧ *fill, complete, amount to*
    ⲘⲈⲌ- prefix to ordinal numbers
ⲘⲞⲨⲌ *burn, flash*
ⲘⲞⲨⲌ *look*
ⲘⲀⲌⲈ m. *cubit*
[ⲘⲀⲀⲌⲈ, ⲘⲀⲌⲈ] v. ⲘⲞⲞϢⲈ *walk*
ⲘⲞⲈⲒⲌⲈ [ⲘⲀⲌⲈⲒⲈ] m.f. *wonder, marvel*
    Ⲣ̄ⲘⲞⲈⲒⲌⲈ *be astonished*
ⲘⲈⲌⲢⲞ m. *manure*
ⲘⲀⲌⲦ, ⲘⲈⲌⲦ m. *bowels, guts, abdomen*
    ⲘⲚ̄ⲦϢⲀⲚⲦⲘⲀⲌⲦ f. *compassion*
Ⲙ̄ⲌⲒⲦ m. *north*
Ⲙ̄ⲌⲀⲀⲨ, Ⲙ̄ⲌⲀⲞⲨ m. *tomb, cave*
ⲘⲀⲀⲬⲈ [ⲘⲀⲬⲈ, ⲘⲈϢⲬⲈ] m. *ear, handle*
ⲘⲀⲀⲬⲈ f. *measure of grain, bushel*
ⲘⲞⲬⲌ, ⲘⲞⲦⲬⲌ m. *belt*
ⲘⲞⲨⲬϬ, ⲘⲞⲨⲬⲔ, ⲘⲞⲨⲬⲦ [ⲘⲞⲨϢϬ], ⲘⲞⲬϬⲧ [ⲘⲀⲬϬⲧ] *be mixed, mix;*
    m. *mixture*

N

called ⲚⲈ   transliterated *n*

Ⲛ̄ as number *fifty*
Final ⲛ at end of line in manuscripts is sometimes dropped and indicated by a
    supralinear stroke.
Ⲛ̄- becomes Ⲙ̄- before [ⲃ], ⲙ, ⲡ, ⲯ, ⲫ
[Ⲛ̄- assimilates before ⲃ, ⲗ, ⲣ]
Ⲛ̄- [ⲚⲚ- before vowels (mainly ⲞⲨ)] genitive preposition *of*
    Ⲛ̄- of attribution (forms adjectives)
Ⲛ̄- [ⲚⲚ- before vowels], Ⲙ̄ⲘⲞⲋ [Ⲙ̄ⲘⲀⲋ] *with, by, in, to, from*
    Ⲛ̄- forms adverbs (Ⲛ̄ⲌⲞⲨⲞ, etc.)
    Ⲛ̄- introduces direct object
    Ⲛ̄- of equivalence (follows ⲟⲧ, ϢⲱⲡⲈ, ϢⲞⲞⲡⲧ and suffix pronouns)
Ⲛ̄-, ⲚⲀⲋ [ⲚⲈⲋ] dative preposition *to, for*
    The paradigm for ⲚⲀⲋ and other presuffixal forms ending in Ⲁⲋ is this:
    ⲚⲀ̈Ⲓ *to me*
    ⲚⲀⲔ *to you* sing. masc.
    ⲚⲈ *to you* sing. fem.
    ⲚⲀϤ *to him*

ⲚⲀⲤ *to her*
ⲚⲀⲚ *to us*
ⲚⲎⲦⲚ̄ *to you* pl.
ⲚⲀⲨ *to them*
Ⲛ̄- . . . ⲀⲚ [often simply . . . ⲀⲚ, . . . ⲈⲚ] negative particles
Ⲛ̄-, ⲚⲈ- definite article plural *the* v. ⲡ-
Ⲛ̄-, Ⲛ̄Ⲧⲋ v. ⲈⲒⲚⲈ *bring*
Ⲛ̄ⲋ conjugation base conjunctive (Ⲛ̄ⲦⲀ-, Ⲛ̄ⲅ-, Ⲛ̄ⲦⲈ-, Ⲛ̄ϥ-, etc.)
-Ⲛ̄ suffix pronoun 1st person pl. *us*
ⲚⲀ, ⲚⲀⲈ [ⲚⲈⲒ] *have pity, mercy;* m. *pity, mercy*
    ⲘⲚ̄ⲦⲚⲀ f. *alms, charity*
    ϢⲀⲀⲦⲘ̄ⲘⲚ̄ⲦⲚⲀⲈ *beg;* m. *beggar*
    ⲚⲀϨⲎⲦ, ⲚⲀⲎⲦ *merciful, compassionate*
ⲚⲀⳋ- [Ⲛ̄ⲚⲀ-, Ⲁ-, ⲚⲈ-] *be going† to* future auxiliary v. ⲚⲞⲨ
    ⲈⲦⲚⲀ- [ⲈⲦⲀ-] relative future *who will*
ⲚⲀ-, ⲚⲈⲋ possessive *those which belong to, of* v. ⲡⲀ- and ⲡⲈⲋ
ⲚⲀⲀ-, ⲚⲀⲈ-, ⲚⲀⲀⲋ [ⲚⲈⲈⲋ, ⲚⲈⲀⲋ] *be great, large* (subj. as suffix)
    ⲚⲀⲓ̈ⲀⲦⲋ *blessed* v. ⲈⲒⲀ
ⲚⲀⲓ̈, ⲚⲈⲓ̈- *these* v. ⲡⲀⲓ̈
ⲚⲈ copular pronoun pl. *they are* v. ⲡⲈ
ⲚⲈ- preterit converter (followed optionally by . . . ⲡⲈ)
    ⲚⲈⲋ [ⲚⲀⲋ], ⲚⲈⲢⲈ- conjugation base imperfect
    ⲚⲈⲋ ⲚⲀ- future imperfect *would have*
[ⲚⲈⲋ] conj. base negative III future v. Ⲛ̄ⲚⲈⲋ
[ⲚⲈⲒ, ⲚⲎⲒⲈ] f. *time*
    †ⲚⲎⲈⲒⲈ *appoint*]
ⲚⲎ demonstrative pronoun pl. *those* v. ⲡⲎ
    ⲚⲒ- demonstrative article pl. v. ⲡⲒ-
ⲚⲞⲨ *go*
    ⲚⲀ† q.v. *be going† to* (used as future auxiliary)
ⲚⲞⲨⲋ [Ⲛⲱⲋ] possessive pronoun pl. *things belonging to* v. ⲡⲱⲋ
[ⲚⲎⲂ, ⲚⲀⲡ, ⲚⲈⲡ] m. *lord*]
ⲚⲞⲨⲂ, ⲚⲞⲨϥ m. *gold, golden*
ⲚⲎⲎⲂⲈ, ⲚⲎⲂⲈ *float, swim*
ⲚⲞⲂⲈ [ⲚⲀⲂⲒ] m. *sin*
    Ⲣ̄ⲚⲞⲂⲈ *sin*
    ⲢⲈϥⲢ̄ⲚⲞⲂⲈ m. *sinner*
ⲚⲞⲨⲂⲦ, ⲚⲞⲂⲦⲋ *weave*
    ⲚⲎⲂⲦⲈ f. *plait, braid*
ⲚⲞⲈⲒⲔ m. *adulterer*
    Ⲣ̄ⲚⲞⲈⲒⲔ *commit adultery*
ⲚⲀⲀⲔⲈ f. *labor pains, agony*
    †ⲚⲀⲀⲔⲈ *be in labor*
Ⲛ̄ⲔⲀ [Ⲛ̄ⲔⲈ] m. *thing, property, belongings*
ⲚⲞⲔⲚⲈⲔ (ⲈϨⲞⲨⲚ Ⲉ-) *have affection*
Ⲛ̄ⲔⲞⲦⲔ, Ⲛ̄ⲔⲞⲦⲈ [Ⲛ̄ⲔⲞⲦ, Ⲛ̄ⲔⲀⲦⲔⲈ] *sleep, lie down;* m. *sleep*
ⲚⲒⲘ *who?*
ⲚⲒⲘ *every, all*
    Ⲛ̄ⲔⲀ ⲚⲒⲘ, ϨⲰⲂ ⲚⲒⲘ *everything*

ⲞⲨⲞⲚ ⲚⲒⲘ *everyone*

ⲚⲀⲘⲈ *truly* v. ⲘⲈ

ⲚⲘ̄ⲘⲀⲞ [ⲚⲘ̄ⲘⲈⲞ] v. Ⲙ̄Ⲛ- *with, and*

ⲚⲞⲘⲦⲈ [ⲚⲀⲘⲦⲈ] f. *strength, power*
[†ⲚⲀⲘⲦⲈ *encourage, comfort*]

[Ⲛ̄Ⲛ- reduplicated Ⲛ̄- before vowels]

ⲚⲞⲈⲒⲚ [ⲚⲀⲈⲒⲚ] *shake, tremble*

ⲚⲞⲨⲚ m.f. *abyss, depth*

ⲚⲀⲚⲞⲨ-, ⲚⲀⲚⲞⲨⲞ *be good* (subj. as suffix)
ⲚⲀⲚⲞⲨⳌ *it is good*
ⲠⲈⲦⲚⲀⲚⲞⲨϥ *good* (substantive, can take def. art. ⲠⲠⲈⲦⲚⲀⲚⲞⲨϥ)
ⲣⲈϥⲣ̄ⲠⲈⲦⲚⲀⲚⲞⲨϥ m. *benefactor*

ⲚⲞⲨⲚⲈ f. *root*

Ⲛ̄ⲚⲈⲞ [ⲚⲈⲞ], Ⲛ̄ⲚⲈ- conjugation base negative III future
Ⲛ̄ⲚⲞ neg. imper. *no!, it will not be so!*

ⲚⲈⲠⲈ- conj. base imperfect v. ⲚⲈ-

Ⲛ̄ⲤⲀ-, Ⲛ̄ⲤⲱⲞ *behind* v. ⲤⲀ

ⲚⲈⲤⲈ-, ⲚⲈⲤⲱⲞ *be beautiful* (subj. as suffix)

ⲚⲈⲤⲂⲱⲱⲞ *be wise* (subj. as suffix, ⲤⲂⲞ)

ⲚⲀⲒ̈ⲀⲦⲞ [ⲚⲈⲈⲒⲈⲦⲞ, ⲚⲈⲈⲒⲀⲦⲞ] *blessed* v. ⲈⲒⲀ

ⲚⲞⲨⲦ, ⲚⲀⲦⲞ *grind, pound* grain
ⲚⲞⲈⲒⲦ m. *meal, flour*

Ⲛ̄ⲦⲞ v. ⲈⲒⲚⲈ *bring*

Ⲛ̄ⲦⲀⲞ, Ⲛ̄ⲦⲀ- conjugation base II perfect

Ⲛ̄ⲦⲀⲞ [Ⲛ̄ⲦⲀ⳾Ⲟ] for ⲈⲚⲦⲀⲞ [ⲈⲚⲦⲀ⳾Ⲟ] relative I perfect, q.v.

Ⲛ̄ⲦⲈ-, Ⲛ̄ⲦⲀⲞ [Ⲛ̄ⲦⲈⲞ] genitive preposition
Ⲛ̄ⲦⲀⲞ indicates possession

Ⲛ̄ⲦⲞ, Ⲛ̄ⲦⲈ- personal pronoun 2nd person sing. fem. *you*

ⲚⲞⲨⲦⲈ m. *God* (mostly with def. art. ⲠⲚⲞⲨⲦⲈ)
f. Ⲛ̄ⲦⲱⲣⲈ *Goddess*, pl. ⲈⲚⲦⲎⲣ *demons*
ⲠⲀⲠⲚⲞⲨⲦⲈ *Paphnutius*, fourth-century monk (belonging to God)
ϢⲈⲚⲞⲨⲦⲈ *Shenute*, fourth-century abbot (son, ϢⲎⲣⲈ, of God)

Ⲛ̄ⲦⲞⲔ [Ⲛ̄ⲦⲀⲔ], Ⲛ̄ⲦⲔ- personal pronoun 2nd person sing. masc. *you*

ⲚⲞⲨⲦⲘ̄, ⲚⲞⲦⲘ̄† *be sweet*

Ⲛ̄ⲦⲚ̄-, Ⲛ̄ⲦⲞⲞⲦⲞ *by, from* v. ⲦⲱⲣⲈ

Ⲛ̄ⲦⲈⲨⲚⲞⲨ *immediately* v. ⲞⲨⲚⲞⲨ

Ⲛ̄ⲦⲈⲣⲈⲞ [Ⲛ̄ⲦⲀⲣⲈⲞ], Ⲛ̄ⲦⲈⲣⲈ- [Ⲛ̄ⲦⲀⲣⲈ-] conjugation base temporal *when, after*

Ⲛ̄ⲦⲞⲤ [Ⲛ̄ⲦⲀⲤ] personal pronoun 3rd person sing. fem. *she, it*

Ⲛ̄ⲦⲞⲞⲦⲞ *by, from* v. ⲦⲱⲣⲈ

Ⲛ̄ⲦⲱⲦⲚ̄ [Ⲛ̄ⲦⲱⲦⲚⲈ], Ⲛ̄ⲦⲈⲦⲚ̄- personal pronoun 2nd person pl. *you*

Ⲛ̄ⲦⲞⲞⲨ [Ⲛ̄ⲦⲀⲨ] personal pronoun 3rd person pl. *they*

Ⲛ̄ⲦⲞⲞⲨⲚ, Ⲛ̄ⲦⲱⲞⲨⲚ *then*

ⲚⲞⲨⲦϥ, ⲚⲈⲦϥ-, ⲚⲈⲦⲂ-, ⲚⲞⲦϥ† *loosen, dissolve, relax*; m. *relaxation*
ⲚⲈⲦϥⲣⲱⲞ *smile*

Ⲛ̄ⲦⲞϥ [Ⲛ̄ⲦⲀϥ] personal pronoun 3rd person sing. masc. *he, it*
Ⲛ̄ⲦⲞϥ [Ⲛ̄ⲦⲀϥ] *but, rather, on the contrary*

[Ⲛ̄ⲦⲀ⳾Ⲟ] v. Ⲛ̄ⲦⲀⲞ conj. base relative I perfect

Ⲛ̄ⲐⲈ (Ⲛ̄-) *like* v. ⳋⲈ

ⲚⲦⲎϬ   m. *plant, weed*

ⲚⲀⲨ [ⲚⲈⲨ] (ⲉ-), imper. ⲀⲚⲀⲨ [ⲈⲚⲀⲨ] *see, look at;* m. *sight, vision*
   ⲚⲀⲨ ⲈⲂⲞⲖ [ⲚⲀⲂⲞⲖ] *see*
   ⲀⲦⲚⲀⲨ ⲈⲢⲞ⸗ *invisible*

ⲚⲀⲨ [ⲚⲈⲨ] m. *hour, time, moment*
   ⲚⲞⲨ *time* of day
   ⲦⲚⲀⲨ *when?*

ⲚⲈⲨ- (for ⲚⲈ- ⲞⲨ) preterit plus indef. art.

ⲚⲎⲨ†, ⲚⲎⲞⲨ† [ⲚⲎⲎⲨ†, Ⲛ̄ⲚⲎⲨ†, Ⲛ̄ⲚⲎⲞⲨ†] *be coming†, about to come†* (serves as
   the qualitative of ⲈⲒ)

[ⲚⲞⲨⲞⲨϨ, ⲚⲞⲞⲨϨ⸗, ⲚⲀⲨϨ⸗, ⲚⲀⲨϨ† *turn, return*]

ⲚⲀϢⲈ-, ⲚⲀϢⲰ⸗ *be many, much, numerous, great* (subj. as suffix)

ⲚⲞⲨϢⲠ, ⲚⲈϢⲠ-, ⲚⲞϢⲠ⸗ *agitate, frighten, shake*

ⲚⲞⲨϢⲤ, ⲚⲞϢⲤ⸗ *grow numb, make numb*
   ⲚⲞϢⲤϤ m. *pugnacious person*

Ⲛ̄ϢⲞⲦ, ⲚⲀϢⲦ† *be hard, strong, difficult;* m. *hardness, boldness*
   ⲘⲚ̄ⲦⲚⲀϢⲦ²ϨⲦ f. *hardheartedness*
   ⲚⲀϢⲦⲈ f. *strength, protector*

ⲚⲈⲈϤ   m. *sailor*

ⲚⲒϤⲈ   *blow, breathe;* m. *breath*

ⲚⲈϤⲢ-, ⲚⲞⲨⲢ⳱† *be good, profitable, useful* (subj. as suffix)
   ⲚⲞϤⲢⲈ [ⲚⲀϤⲢⲈ] f. *good, profit, advantage*
   Ⲣ̄ⲚⲞϤⲢⲈ *be profitable*
   ⲚⲞⲨϤⲈ *good*

ⲚⲈϨ, ⲚⲎϨ   m. *oil*
   ⲚⲈϨⲘⲈ *genuine* (ⲘⲈ) *oil, olive oil*

ⲚⲞⲨϨ   m. *rope, cord*

ⲚⲞⲨϨⲈ, ⲚⲈϨ-, ⲚⲀϨ⸗, ⲚⲎϨ†, ⲚⲈϨ† *shake off, separate*

ⲚⲞⲨϨⲈ   f. *sycamore*

ⲚⲞⲨϨⲂ̄, ⲚⲀϨⲂ⸗, ⲚⲀϨⲂ̄† *yoke*
   ⲚⲀϨⲂ̄, ⲚⲀϨⲂⲈϤ m. *yoke*
   ⲚⲀϨⲂ̄, ⲚⲀϨⲂⲈ f. *shoulders, back*

ⲚⲞⲨϨⲂ̄   *copulate, impregnate*

ⲚⲞⲨϨⲘ̄ [ⲚⲞⲨϨⲘⲈ], ⲚⲀϨⲘ⸗ *be saved, save, rescue*

ⲚⲈϨⲚⲞⲨϨ⸗, ⲚⲈϨⲚⲞⲨϨ† *shake*

ⲚⲈϨⲠⲈ   *mourn;* m. *mourning*

ⲚⲀϨⲢⲚ̄- [Ⲛ̄ⲚⲀϨⲢⲚ̄-], ⲚⲀϨⲢⲀ⸗ [Ⲛ̄ⲚⲀϨⲢⲀ⸗, ⲚⲀϨⲢⲈ⸗] *in presence of, before*
   v. ϨⲞ

ⲚⲈϨⲤⲈ   *awaken, arise*

Ⲛ̄ϨⲎⲦ⸗ v. Ϩ̄Ⲛ̄- *in*

ⲚⲀϨⲦⲈ, [Ⲛ̄ϨⲞⲨⲦ⸗], Ⲛ̄ϨⲞⲦ† *trust, believe, be trustworthy†, genuine;* m. *trust,
   faith*
   ⲀⲦⲚⲀϨⲦⲈ *unbelieving*
   ⲘⲚ̄ⲦⲀⲦⲚⲀϨⲦⲈ f. *unbelief*

ⲚⲞⲨϪ   *lying, false*

ⲚⲞⲨϪⲈ, ⲚⲈϪ- [ⲚⲞⲨϪ-], ⲚⲞϪ⸗ [ⲚⲀϪ⸗], ⲚⲎϪ† *throw, toss, cast, lie†, be
   reclining†*
   ⲚⲞⲨϪⲈ ⲈⲂⲞⲖ *cast out, throw away, discard*

ⲚⲞⲨϪⲔ   *sprinkle, asperge, scatter*

ⲚⲀⲬϨⲈ,ⲚⲀⲀⲬⲈ f. *tooth*
ⲚⲞϬ [ⲚⲀϬ] *great, large, big*, n. *great* person, *old* person or thing
ⲚϬⲒ- [Ⲛ̄ⲬⲈ-,Ⲛ̄ⲬⲒ-] indicates subject *namely* (usually left untranslated)
ⲚⲈϬⲰ⳽ *be ugly, disgusting* (subj. as suffix)
ⲚⲞϬⲚⲈϬ [ⲚⲀϬⲚϬ],ⲚⲈϬⲚⲞⲨϬ⳽ *insult, mock;* m. *abuse, insult*
ⲚⲞⲨϬⲤ [ⲚⲞⲨϬⲈ],ⲚⲞϬⲤ† *be angry;* m. *anger*

ⲝ
called ⲝⲓ transliterated *ks*

ⲝ̄ as number *sixty*
ⲝ̄ for ⲕⲥ

ⲟ
called ⲟⲩ transliterated *o*

ⲟ̄ as number *seventy*
[ⲟ is sometimes replaced by ⲁ]
-ⲟ, -ⲱ, -ⲟⲩ *great, large* in ⲉⲓⲉⲣⲟ, ⲣ̄ⲣⲟ, Ϩⲗ̄ⲗⲟ, etc. (cf. ⲁⲓ̈ⲁⲓ̈)
ⲟ† [ⲟⲉⲓⲧ] *be†* v. ⲉⲓⲣⲉ
ⲟⲓ̈† *be great†* v. ⲁⲓ̈ⲁⲓ̈
ⲟⲂⲈ† v. ⲉⲓⲂⲈ *be thirsty*
ⲟⲂϢ⳽,ⲟⲂϢ† v. ⲱⲂϢ *forget*
ⲟⲂϨⲈ f. *tooth*
ⲟⲈⲒⲔ m. *bread*
ⲟⲘⲈ m.f. *clay, mud*
    ⲟⲨⲀⲘⲟⲘⲈ f. *earth-eating animal, eater, ulcer, gangrene*
ⲟⲈⲒⲘⲈ,ⲟⲈⲒⲘ f. *hook*
ⲟⲚ [ⲀⲚ] *once again, also, still, yet, additionally, moreover*
ⲟⲚϨ†, ⲟⲚⲀϨ† v. ⲱⲚϨ *live*
ⲟⲢⲬ† v. ⲱⲢⲬ *be firm*
ⲟⲤⲈ [ⲀⲤⲈ,ⲀⲤⲒ] m. *loss, damage*
    †ⲟⲤⲈ· *suffer loss, be fined, forfeit*
ⲟⲤⲔ† v. ⲱⲤⲔ *delay*
ⲟⲟⲦ† *groan*
ⲟⲟⲦⲈ [ⲀⲦⲈ],ⲦⲟⲦⲈ [ⲦⲈⲦⲈ] f. *womb, vagina*
ⲟϢ† v. ⲁϢⲁⲓ̈ *become many*
ⲟϢ⳽ v. ⲱϢ *read*
ⲟⲈⲒϢ [ⲀⲈⲒϢ] n. *cry, call*
    ⲦⲀϢⲈⲟⲈⲒϢ *proclaim* v. ⲦⲀϢⲈ-
[ⲟϢⲉ†] v. ⲉⲓϢⲉ *hang*
ⲟϢⲘ⳽,ⲟϢⲘ̄† v. ⲱϢⲘ̄ *be quenched*
ⲟⲟϨ m. *moon*
ⲟϨⲈ,ⲱϨⲈ m. *sheepfold, cattle pen, pasture, flock, herd*
ⲟϨⲤ *sickle* v. ⲱϨⲤ

ⲡ
called ⲡⲓ transliterated *p*

ⲡ as number *eighty*
ⲡ- definite article sing. masc., fem ⲧ-, pl. ⲛ̄- *the*
    [ⲡ- is sometimes omitted before words having initial ⲡ]
    ⲡⲉ-, ⲧⲉ-, ⲛⲉ- full forms used before double consonants and words for time
    ⲡ- vocative *O!*
ⲡⲁ-, ⲧⲁ-, ⲛⲁ- possessive pronoun *that which belongs to, those which belong to*
ⲡⲁï [ⲡⲉï, ⲡⲉⲉⲓ], ⲧⲁï [ⲧⲉï, ⲧⲉⲉⲓ], ⲛⲁï [ⲛⲉï, ⲛⲉⲉⲓ] demonstrative pronoun
    m., f., pl. *this, these*
    ⲡⲉï-, ⲧⲉï-, ⲛⲉï- demonstrative article m., f., pl. *this, these*
ⲡⲉⲕ, ⲧⲉⲕ, ⲛⲉⲕ possessive article
    The paradigm for possession of a masc. thing is this:
    ⲡⲁ- *my*
    ⲡⲉⲕ- *your* m.
    ⲡⲟⲩ- [ⲡⲉ-] *your* f.
    ⲡⲉϥ- [ⲡϥ̄-] *his*
    ⲡⲉⲥ- *her*
    ⲡⲉⲛ- [ⲡⲛ̄-] *our*
    ⲡⲉⲧⲛ̄- *your* pl.
    ⲡⲉⲩ- [ⲡⲟⲩ-] *their*
    (likewise with ⲧⲉⲕ for possession of a feminine thing and ⲛⲉⲕ for possession of several things)
ⲡⲉ used optionally after preterit converter (ⲛⲉ- . . . ⲡⲉ)
ⲡⲉ, ⲧⲉ, ⲛⲉ copular pronoun m., f., pl. *he, she, it is, they are*
    ⲡⲉⲧ- (ⲡⲉ fused with relative ⲉⲧ- to form cleft sentence) *it is . . . who*
ⲡⲉ, pl. ⲡⲏⲩⲉ f. *heaven, sky*
ⲡⲉⲓ, ⲡⲓ f. *kiss*
    †ⲡⲓ *kiss*
ⲡⲏ, ⲧⲏ, ⲛⲏ demonstrative pronoun m., f., pl. *that, those*
    ⲡⲓ-, †-, ⲛⲓ- demonstrative or affective article *that, those* (often *this, these*),
    [*the*]
ⲡⲱⲕ, ⲧⲱⲕ, ⲛⲟⲩⲕ [ⲛⲱⲕ] absolute possessive pronoun *mine,* etc.
ⲡⲁⲕⲉ, ⲡⲟⲕⲉ†, ⲡⲟⲕ† *be light, shrink*
ⲡⲱⲗϩ, ⲡⲟⲗϩ, ⲡⲟⲗϩ† *wound, be wounded;* m. *wound*
ⲡⲱⲗϭ, ⲡⲱⲗⲕ, ⲡⲁⲗϭ-, ⲡⲟⲗϭ *agree, decide, be satisfied*
    ⲡⲱⲗϭ ⲉⲃⲟⲗ *reach a conclusion, settle*
ⲡⲭϭⲉ m. *torn cloth, rag, worn, old*
ⲡⲱⲛ, ⲡⲱⲱⲛ, ⲡⲱⲱⲛⲉ, ⲡⲉⲛ-, ⲡⲟⲛ, ⲡⲁⲛ, ⲡⲏⲛ† *be poured, flow, pour*
ⲡⲁⲱⲛⲉ name of 10th Egyptian month
ⲡⲱⲱⲛⲉ, ⲡⲉⲉⲛⲉ-, ⲡⲟⲟⲛⲉ [ⲡⲁⲛⲉ], ⲡⲟⲟⲛⲉ† *change, turn, move;*
    m. *removal, death*
    ⲡⲱⲱⲛⲉ ⲉⲃⲟⲗ *move out, leave*
    ⲡⲱⲱⲛⲉ ⲉⲃⲟⲗ ⲛ̄-, ϩⲓ-, ϩⲛ̄- *carry out from*
ⲡⲱⲛⲕ, ⲡⲛ̄ⲅ-, ⲡⲟⲛⲕ *draw, bail water, transfer, carry*
[ⲡⲉⲛⲓⲡⲉ] v. ⲃⲉⲛⲓⲡⲉ *iron*
ⲡⲁⲟⲡⲉ name of 2nd Egyptian month

ⲡⲉⲓⲣⲉ, ⲡⲓⲣⲉ, ⲡⲣ̄ⲣⲉ [ⲡⲣ̄ⲣⲓⲉ], ⲡⲟⲣⲉ†, ⲡⲣⲉⲓⲱⲟⲩ† [ⲡⲣ̄ⲣⲓⲱⲟⲩ†] come forth,
      blossom, shine, radiate; m. shining forth
      ⲙⲁⲙ̄ⲡⲉⲓⲣⲉ m. east
ⲡⲱⲱⲣⲉ, ⲡⲉⲣⲉ- [ⲡⲣ̄ⲣⲉ-, ⲡⲣ̄-], ⲡⲟⲟⲣⲟ dream
      ⲡⲉⲣⲉⲣⲁⲥⲟⲩ dream a dream
ⲡⲣⲱ f. winter
ⲡⲟⲣⲕ in ⲙⲁⲥⲡⲟⲣⲕ wagon
ⲡⲱⲣⲕ, ⲡⲣⲕ-, ⲡⲟⲣⲕⲟ be plucked, destroyed, uproot, pluck
ⲡⲁⲣⲙⲟⲩⲧⲉ name of 8th Egyptian month
ⲡⲁⲣⲉⲙϩⲟⲧⲡ name of 7th Egyptian month
ⲡⲱⲣϣ, ⲡⲣ̄ϣ-, ⲡⲟⲣϣⲟ [ⲡⲁⲣⲉϣⲟ], ⲡⲟⲣϣ† [ⲡⲁⲣϣ†] spread, stretch, be
      spread
      ⲡⲣⲏϣ m. something spread: mat, mattress, bedding, cloak
ⲡⲱⲣⲝ, ⲡⲣ̄ⲝ-, ⲡⲟⲣⲝⲟ [ⲡⲁⲣⲝⲟ], ⲡⲟⲣⲝ† [ⲡⲁⲣⲝ†] divide, separate;
      m. division
ⲡⲓⲥⲉ, ⲡⲉⲥ-, ⲡⲁⲥⲧⲟ, ⲡⲟⲥⲉ† be cooked, melted, boil, bake, melt
ⲯⲓⲥ, ⲯⲓⲧ [ⲡⲥⲉⲓⲧ], f. ⲯⲓⲧⲉ, -ⲯⲓⲧⲉ nine
      ⲯⲧⲁⲓⲟⲩ, ⲯⲁⲓⲧ- [ⲡⲥⲧⲉ-] ninety
ⲡⲁⲧ [ⲡⲉⲧ] f. knee
ⲡⲉⲧ- substantivized relative v. ⲉⲧ-, or in cleft sentence v. ⲡⲉ
ⲡⲱⲧ, ⲡⲏⲧ† run, flee, go, be running†; m. flight
      ⲡⲱⲧ ⲉⲃⲟⲗ ϩⲏⲧⲟ ⲛ̄- run away from
      ⲡⲱⲧ ⲛ̄ⲥⲁ-, ⲛ̄ⲥⲱⲟ pursue, persecute
ⲡⲓⲧⲉ f. bow
ⲡⲱⲧⲥ, ⲡⲟⲧⲥ† divide, split
      ⲡⲁⲧⲥⲉ f. board
ⲡⲟⲟⲩ today v. ϩⲟⲟⲩ
[ⲡⲁⲩⲣⲉ grow; m. growth]
ⲡⲁϣ [ⲡⲁϣⲥϥ] m. trap
ⲡⲱϣ, ⲡⲱϣⲉ, ⲡⲉϣ-, ⲡⲟϣⲟ [ⲡⲁϣⲟ], ⲡⲏϣ† be divided, divide, share, break,
      be split†; m. division
      ⲡⲁϣⲉ f. half
ⲡⲱϣⲛ̄, ⲡⲟϣⲛ̄ⲟ, ⲡⲟϣⲛ̄† serve, ordain; m. service
ⲡⲁϣⲟⲛⲥ name of 9th Egyptian month
ⲡⲱϣⲥ, ⲡⲟϣⲥⲟ, ⲡⲟϣⲥ† be amazed, deranged, amaze; m. amazement
ⲡⲱϩ, ⲡⲁϩ-, ⲡⲁϩⲟ, ⲡⲏϩ† break, burst, tear
ⲡⲱϩ, ⲡⲉϩ-, ⲡⲏϩ† reach, attain, succeed, ripen, befit(?)
      ⲡϩⲛ̄- as vb. aux. succeed in, when once
ⲡⲁϩⲣⲉ m. drug, remedy, medicine
      ⲣ̄ⲡⲁϩⲣⲉ, †ⲡⲁϩⲣⲉ use or give drugs, treat, cure
      ⲙⲛ̄ⲧⲣⲉϥⲣ̄ⲡⲁϩⲣⲉ f. sorcery
ⲡⲱϩⲥ, ⲡⲉϩⲥ-, ⲡⲁϩⲥⲟ, ⲡⲟϩⲥ† bite; m. bite
ⲡⲱϩⲧ, ⲡⲉϩⲧ-, ⲡⲁϩⲧⲟ, ⲡⲁϩⲧ† bend oneself, fall, kneel, lie prostrate
      also means pour, flow
      ⲡⲱϩⲧ ⲉⲃⲟⲗ pour forth, shed
ⲡⲁϩⲟⲩ m. rear, behind, backside
      ⲉⲡⲁϩⲟⲩ ⲛ̄-, ⲙ̄ⲙⲟⲟ behind, backward
      ϩⲓⲡⲁϩⲟⲩ ⲛ̄-, ⲙ̄ⲙⲟⲟ behind, after
ⲡⲉⲝⲉ-, ⲡⲉⲝⲁⲟ [ⲡⲁⲝⲉⲟ] said (subj. as suffix) used in introducing

quotations
ⲡⲉϫⲁϥ ϫⲉ *he said, " . . . "*
ⲡϫⲱ m. *poison*
ⲡⲱϫϭ, ⲡⲟϫⲧ† *beat flat;* m. *flat part, breadth*
ⲡⲁϭⲥⲉ f. *saliva*
   ⲛⲉϫⲡⲁϭⲥⲉ *spit* (ⲛⲟⲩϫⲉ)

Ⲣ
called ⲣⲱ   transliterated *r*

ⲣ̅ as number *one hundred*
[ⲣ̅- can stand for ⲛ̅-]
ⲣ̅- v. ⲉⲓⲣⲉ *do*
ⲣⲁ m. *state, condition*
  ⲣⲁⲕⲟⲧⲉ *Alexandria*
  ⲣⲁⲧⱳⲃⲉ m. *joint* (ⲧⲱⲃⲉ)
  ⳅⲁⲡⲣⲁ ⲛ̅- *as to, about, concerning*
ⲣⲁ-, ⲣⲉ- m. *part, fraction*
  ⲣⲉⲙⲏⲧ *one tenth*
ⲣⲏ m. *sun*
ⲣⲓ f. *room, monk's cell*
ⲣⲟ, ⲣⲁ-, ⲣⲱ⸗, pl. ⲣⲱⲟⲩ m. *mouth, door*
  ⲉⲣⲛ̅-, ⲉⲣⲱ⸗ *to, upon, at*
  ⲕⲁⲣⲱ⸗, ⲕⲁⲣⲁⲉⲓⲧ† *be silent* (ⲕⲱ)
  ⲕⲁⲣⲱϥ m. *silence*
  ⳅⲁⲣⲛ̅-, ⳅⲁⲣⲱ⸗ *beneath, before*
  ⳅⲓⲣⲛ̅-, ⳅⲓⲣⲱ⸗ *at, upon*
ⲣⲱ *indeed, even, but, at all*
ⲣ̅ⲃⲉ *enclosure* v. ⱳⲣⲃ̅
ⲣⲓⲕⲉ, ⲣⲉⲕⲧ-, ⲣⲉⲕ-, ⲣⲉⲕⲧ⸗ [ⲣⲁⲕⲧ⸗], ⲣⲟⲕⲉ†, ⲣⲁⲕⲉ†, ⲣⲁⲕⲧⲉ† *bend, turn, incline;* m. *inclination*
  ⲣⲁⲕⲧⲥ f. *direction, perversion*
ⲣⲉⲕⲣⲓⲕⲉ f. *nodding* with drowsiness
ⲣⲁⲕⲟⲧⲉ *Alexandria* v. ⲣⲁ
ⲣⲱⲕⳅ, ⲣⲟⲕⳅ⸗, ⲣⲁⲕⳅ⸗, ⲣⲟⲕⳅ† *burn;* m. *fire*
ⲣⲓⲙⲉ *cry, weep;* m. *weeping*
  ⲣ̅ⲙⲉⲓⲏ [ⲣ̅ⲙ̅ⲙⲉⲓⲏ], pl. ⲣ̅ⲙⲉⲓⲟⲟⲩⲉ f. *tear*
ⲣⲱⲙⲉ, ⲣⲙ̅- m.f. *person, one, human being*
  ⲣⲙ̅ⲛ̅- *person of, one from*
  ⲣⲉϥ- [ⲣ̅ⲙⲉϥ-, ⲣⲱⲙⲉϥ-, ⲣ̅ⲙ̅ⲙⲉϥ-, f. ⲣⲉⲥ-] *one who, thing which, -er*
  ⲣⲙ̅ⲙⲁⲟ, [pl. ⲣ̅ⲙ̅ⲙⲁⲉⲓ] m.f. *rich person, rich* (-ⲟ)
  ⲙⲛ̅ⲧⲣⲙ̅ⲙⲁⲟ f. *riches, wealth*
ⲣⲟⲙⲡⲉ [ⲣⲁⲙⲡⲉ], ⲣ̅ⲙⲡⲉ-, pl. ⲣ̅ⲙ̅ⲡⲟⲟⲩⲉ f. *year*
  ⲧⲛ̅ⲣⲟⲙⲡⲉ, ⲧⲣ̅ⲣⲟⲙⲡⲉ *each year, annually*
ⲣⲙ̅ⳅⲉ, f. ⲣⲙ̅ⳅⲏ, pl. ⲣⲙ̅ⳅⲉⲉⲩⲉ m. *free person*
  ⲙⲛ̅ⲧⲣⲙ̅ⳅⲉ f. *freedom*
ⲣⲁⲛ [ⲣⲉⲛ], ⲣⲉⲛ-, ⲣⲛ̅ⲧ⸗, ⲣⲓⲛ⸗ [ⲣⲛ̅⸗] m. *name*
  ϯⲣⲉⲛ⸗ *call*

ṖΠ- v. ΗΡΠ   *wine*
ṖΠΕ [ΕΡΠΕ, ṖΠΕΕΙ], pl. ṖΠΗΥΕ   m. *temple*
ΡΙΡ   m. *pig*
ṖΡΟ, ΕΡΟ, f. ṖΡΩ, ΕΡΩ, pl. ṖΡΩΟΥ [ṖΡΑΕΙ]   m. *king, caesar, emperor,*
    f. *queen*
    ΜΝ̄ΤṖΡΟ, ΜΝ̄ΤΕΡΟ   f. *kingdom, reign*
    ṖṖΡΟ   *reign*
ṖΡΗΤ v. ΕΡΗΤ   *vow*
ΡΗC   m. *south*
    ΜΑΡΗC   m. *Upper Egypt*
ΡΟΕΙC [ΡΑΕΙC], ΡΗC†   *be awake, watch*; m. *guard*
ṖCΩ, pl. ṖCΟΟΥΕ   f. *animal pen*
ΡΑCΤΕ   m. *tomorrow, the following day*
ΡΑCΟΥ [ΡΕCΟΥΕ]   f. *dream*
ΡΑΤ⸗ [ΡΕΤ⸗]   m. *foot of* (only in compounds, cf. ΟΥΕΡΗΤΕ)
    Ν̄ΡΑΤ⸗   *trace* (ΕΙΝΕ)
    ΑΤΝ̄ΡΑΤ⸗   *untraceable, inscrutable*
    ϬΝ̄ΡΑΤ⸗   *search*
    ΕΡΑΤ⸗ [ΑΡΕΤ⸗]   *to*
    ϨΑΡΑΤ⸗   *beneath*
    ϨΙΡΑΤ⸗   *toward*
ΡΩΤ, ΡΕΤ-, ΡΗΤ†, p.c. ΡΑΤ-   *grow, sprout, bring forth*
ΡΑϊΤΕ   f. *relatives, family*
[ΡΗΤΕ   m. *manner*
    Μ̄ΠΙΡΗΤΕ   *thus*
    Μ̄ΠΡΗΤΕ Ν̄-   *like, in the manner of*]
ΡΑΥΗ   f. *neighborhood*
ΡΟΟΥΕ   m. *stubble, straw*
ΡΟΟΥΝΕ   m. *virgin*
ΡΟΟΥΤ† v. ΟΥΡΟΤ   *be glad*
ΡΟΟΥϢ [ΡΑΟΥϢ]   m. *care, concern, anxiety*
    ṖΡΟΟΥϢ   *be anxious*
    ϤΙΡΟΟΥϢ   *be concerned, care*
ΡΑϢ in ΡΜ̄ΡΑϢ   m.f. *mild, gentle person*
    ΜΝ̄ΤΡΜ̄ΡΑϢ   f. *gentleness*
ΡΑϢΕ [ΡΕϢΕ]   *rejoice*; m. *joy*
    ΡΑϢΕ Ν̄-, Μ̄ΜΟ⸗   *rejoice at, in*
ΡΩϢΕ, ΡΕϢΤ-, ΡΑϢΤ⸗   *suffice, be responsible, content*; m. *enough, plenty*
ṖϢΩΝ   m. *cloak, covering*
ΡΑϢΡΕϢ, ΡΕϢΡΕϢ†   *flourish*
ΡΕϤ-   *one who* v. ΡΩΜΕ
ΡΟΥϨΕ   m. *evening*
    ϨΙΡΟΥϨΕ   n. *evening*
ΡΩϨΕ, ΡΑϨΕ†   *wash*
ΡΩϨΤ, ΡΕϨΤ-, ΡΑϨΤ⸗, ΡΑϨΤ†   *strike, be struck†, hit, throw*
ΡΑϨΤΕ, ΡΟϨΤΕ   f. *kettle, cauldron*

C
called ϭⲏⲙⲙⲁ   transliterated *s*

ⲥ̄   as number *two hundred*
ⲥ-   personal pronoun 3rd person sing. fem. *she, it*
-ⲥ   suffix pronoun 3rd person sing. fem. *her, it*
ⲥⲁ   m. *side, part, direction*
    ⲛ̄ⲥⲁ- [ⲥⲉ-], ⲛ̄ⲥⲱ⸗   *behind, after, at*
    ⲛ̄ⲥⲁ-, ⲛ̄ⲥⲱ⸗   *except*
    ⲛ̄ⲥⲁⲃⲏⲗ ⲉ- [ⲥⲁⲃⲗ̄ⲗⲉ⸗]   *except*
    ⲛ̄ⲥⲁⲃⲏⲗ ⲭⲉ-   *except, unless*
    ⲙⲛ̄ⲛ̄ⲥⲁ-, ⲙⲛ̄ⲛ̄ⲥⲱ⸗   temporal *after*
    ⲙⲛ̄ⲛ̄ⲥⲁⲧⲣⲉ-   *after*
    ⲙⲛ̄ⲛ̄ⲥⲱⲥ   *afterwards*
ⲥⲁ   *be beautiful*; [ⲥⲁⲉⲓⲉ] m. *beauty*
    ⲥⲁⲉⲓⲉ   m. *beautiful person, beautiful*
ⲥⲁ ⲛ̄-   m. *person of, dealer, seller*
ⲥⲉ   *yes*
ⲥⲉ   *sixty* v. ⲥⲟⲟⲩ
ⲥⲉ-   personal pronoun 3rd person pl. *they*
-ⲥⲉ, -ⲥⲟⲩ   suffix pronoun 3rd person pl. *them*
ⲥⲉⲓ, ⲥⲓ, ⲥⲏⲩ†   *be filled, satisfied*; m. *satiety, overindulgence*
    ⲙⲛ̄ⲧⲁⲧⲥⲓ   f. *greed*
ⲥⲟ   in †ⲥⲟ   *spare, refrain*; m. *hindrance*
ⲥⲟ, ⲥⲟⲉ v. ⲥⲟⲟⲩ   *six*
ⲥⲟⲓ̈ [ⲥⲟⲉⲓ]   m.f. *beam of wood*
    ⲟⲩⲉϩⲥⲟⲓ̈   f. *roof, rafters* (ⲟⲩⲱϩ)
ⲥⲱ, ⲥⲉ-, ⲥⲟⲟ⸗, p.c. ⲥⲁⲩ-   *drink*; m. *drinking, drink*
    ⲥⲱⲱϥ   pl. *drinking*
ⲥⲁⲃⲉ, f. ⲥⲁⲃⲏ, pl. ⲥⲁⲃⲉⲉⲩ   m. *wise person*
    ⲥⲃⲟ   *learn* v. ⲧⲥⲁⲃⲟ
    ⲥⲃⲟⲩⲓ̈   m. *disciple, pupil*
    ⲥⲃⲱ, pl. ⲥⲃⲟⲟⲩⲉ [ⲥⲃⲟⲩ]   f. *doctrine, teaching*
    †ⲥⲃⲱ   *teach*, cf. ⲧⲥⲁⲃⲟ
    ⲭⲓⲥⲃⲱ   *learn*
ⲥⲏⲃⲉ, ⲥⲏϥⲉ   f. *reed, flute, shin bone*
ⲥⲱⲃⲉ   *laugh, mock*; m. *laughter, object of ridicule*
    ⲥⲱⲃⲉ ⲛ̄ⲥⲁ-   *laugh at, make fun of*
ⲥⲃ̄ⲃⲉ, ⲥⲃ̄ⲃⲉ-, ⲥⲃ̄ⲃⲏⲧ†, ⲥⲃ̄ⲃⲏⲩ†, ⲥⲃ̄ⲃⲏⲩⲧ†   *circumcise, be circumcised*;
    m. *circumcision*
    ⲙⲛ̄ⲧⲁⲧⲥⲃ̄ⲃⲉ   f. *uncircumcision*
ⲥⲃⲟⲕ, ⲥⲟⲃⲕ† [ⲥⲁⲃⲕ†, ⲥⲁⲃⲉⲕ†]   *become small, few*; m. *smallness, few*
ⲥⲓⲃⲧ   f. *hill*
ⲥⲟⲃⲧ [ⲥⲁⲃⲧ]   m. *wall, fence*
ⲥⲟⲃⲧⲉ [ⲥⲁⲃⲧⲉ], ⲥⲟϥⲧⲉ, ⲥⲃ̄ⲧⲉ-, ⲥⲃ̄ⲧⲱⲧ⸗, ⲥⲃ̄ⲧⲱⲧ†   *prepare, be ready*†;
    m. *equipment, preparation*
ⲥⲱⲃϩ, ⲥⲟⲃϩ-, ⲥⲟⲃϩ⸗, ⲥⲟⲃϩ†   *have leprosy, be a leper*†; m. *leprosy*
ⲥⲱⲕ, ⲥⲉⲕ-, ⲥⲟⲕ⸗ [ⲥⲁⲕ⸗], ⲥⲏⲕ†   *draw, pull, gather, be drawn*, also means *flow,*
    glide

ⲥⲱⲕ ϩⲏⲧ⸗ *lead*
ⲥⲓⲕⲉ, ⲥⲁⲕⲧ⸗, ⲥⲟⲕⲉ† *grind, pound*
ⲥⲕⲁï, ⲥⲉⲕ-, ⲥⲟⲕ⸗ *plow*
ⲥⲕⲟⲣⲕⲣ̄, ⲥⲕⲣ̄ⲕⲣ̄- *roll, be rolled*; m. *rolling*
ⲥⲟⲗ m. *wick*
ⲥⲱⲗ, ⲥⲏⲗ† *corrupt*
ⲥⲱⲗⲡ, ⲥⲗⲡ-, ⲥⲟⲗⲡ⸗, ⲥⲟⲗⲡ† *break, burst, be broken, cut off*
ⲥⲗⲟⲡⲗⲉⲡ [ⲥⲗⲁⲡⲗⲡ] *tear apart*
ⲥⲟⲗⲥⲗ̄, ⲥⲗ̄ⲥⲗ̄-, ⲥⲗ̄ⲥⲱⲗ⸗ *comfort*; m. *consolation*
ⲥⲗⲁⲁⲧⲉ [ⲥⲗⲁⲧⲉ, ⲥⲗⲟⲟⲧⲉ] *stumble, slip*; m. *stumbling*
ⲥⲗ̄ϩⲟ in ⲙⲟⲩⲛ̄ⲥⲗ̄ϩⲟ *lukewarm water*
ⲥⲱⲗϭ [ⲥⲱⲗⲉϫ] *smear, obliterate*
ⲥⲗⲟϭⲗϭ, ⲥⲗⲉϭⲗⲱϭ† *be smooth, make smooth*
ⲥⲓⲙ m. *grass, hay*
ⲥⲱⲙ, ⲥⲟⲙ⸗, ⲥⲏⲙ† *pound, press*
ⲥⲙⲏ f. *voice*
    ϫⲓⲥⲙⲏ *listen*
ⲥⲙⲟⲩ, ⲥⲙⲁⲙⲁⲁⲧ† *bless, praise, be blessed*†; m. *blessing, praise*
ⲥⲙ̄ⲙⲉ *appeal;* m. *petition*
    ⲥⲙ̄ⲙⲉ ⲉ- *accuse*
    ⲁⲛⲥⲙ̄ⲙⲉ n. *ordinance*
    ϯⲁⲛⲥⲙ̄ⲙⲉ *command*
ⲥⲙⲓⲛⲉ [ⲥⲙ̄ⲛⲉ], ⲥⲙⲛ̄-, ⲥⲙⲛ̄ⲧ⸗, ⲥⲙⲟⲛⲧ† [ⲥⲙⲁⲛⲧ†] *be established, be correct*†, *establish, set in order, lay, compose;* m. *confirmation*
[ⲥⲟⲙⲥ *look*]
ⲥⲱⲙⲧ, ⲥⲱⲙⲛⲧ, ⲥⲟⲙⲧ⸗, ⲥⲟⲙⲧ† *stretch, strain, wait*
ⲥⲙⲟⲧ [ⲥⲙⲁⲧ] m. *form, pattern, manner*
    ⲛ̄ⲕⲉⲥⲙⲟⲧ *otherwise*
    ⲟ ⲛ̄ⲥⲙⲟⲧ *be like*
ⲥⲙⲁϩ m. *bunch*
ⲥⲁⲉⲓⲛ [ⲥⲉⲉⲓⲛ, ⲥⲟⲉⲓⲛ] m. *physician*
ⲥⲟⲛ [ⲥⲁⲛ], pl. ⲥⲛⲏⲩ [ⲥⲛⲏⲟⲩ] m. *brother*
    ⲥⲱⲛⲉ f. *sister*
ⲥⲏⲛⲉ f. *granary*
ⲥⲓⲛⲉ, ⲥⲛ̄-, ⲥⲁⲁⲧ⸗ *pass by, pass through, across*
ⲥⲟⲟⲛⲉ m. *robber*
ⲥⲱⲛⲕ *suck*
ⲥⲛⲁⲉⲓⲛ *jump around, wander about*
ⲥⲛ̄ⲥⲛ̄ *resound*
ⲥⲱⲛⲧ, ⲥⲱⲱⲛⲧ [ⲥⲁⲁⲛⲧ⸗], ⲥⲛ̄ⲧ-, ⲥⲟⲛⲧ⸗ [ⲥⲁⲁⲛⲧ⸗], ⲥⲟⲛⲧ† *be created, create;* m. *creation, creature*
    ϣⲁⲥⲱⲛⲧ *first creation*
    ⲥⲛ̄ⲧⲉ f. *foundation*
ⲥⲱⲛⲧ m. *custom*
ⲥⲟⲛⲧⲉ m. *resin*
ⲥⲛⲁⲩ [ⲥⲛⲉⲩ], f. ⲥⲛ̄ⲧⲉ, -ⲥⲛⲟⲟⲩⲥ m. *two*
    ⲙ̄ⲡⲉⲥⲛⲁⲩ, f. ⲛ̄ⲧⲥⲛ̄ⲧⲉ *both together*
    ⲙⲉϩⲥⲛⲁⲩ *second* (ⲙⲟⲩϩ)
    ⲙⲛ̄ⲧⲥⲛⲟⲟⲩⲥ *twelve* (ⲙⲏⲧ)

ⲥⲁⲁⲛ̄ⲱ [ⲥⲁⲛⲉⲱ, ⲥⲟⲛⲱ], ⲥⲁⲛⲟⲩⲱ⸗, ⲥⲁⲛⲁⲱⲧ† *nourish, rear, well fed*†

ⲥⲛⲟϥ [ⲥⲛⲁϥ] m. *blood*

ⲥⲛⲟⲩϥ n. *last year*

ⲥⲱⲛϩ, ⲥⲟⲛϩ⸗ [ⲥⲁⲛϩ⸗], ⲥⲟⲛϩ† [ⲥⲁⲛϩ†] *bind, be bound*
ⲥⲛⲁⲩϩ [ⲥⲛⲁϩ], pl. ⲥⲛⲟⲟⲩϩ [ⲥⲛⲁⲟⲩϩ] m. *bond, fetter*

ⲥⲡ-, ⲥⲉⲡ- f. *year*

ⲥⲟⲡ [ⲥⲁⲡ], ⲥⲡ-, ⲥⲉⲡ-, ⲥⲱⲡ, ⲥⲱⲱⲡ m. *occasion, time*
ⲟⲩⲥⲟⲡ *one time*
ϩⲓⲟⲩⲥⲟⲡ *together*
ⲥⲉⲡⲥⲛⲁⲩ *twice* (ⲥⲉⲡ- is used with two)
ⲙ̄ⲡⲙⲉϩⲥⲉⲡⲥⲛⲁⲩ *for a second time*
ⲛ̄ϣⲙⲛ̄ⲧⲥⲱⲱⲡ *three times* (ⲥⲱⲱⲡ is used with three)
ⲛ̄ⲕⲉⲥⲟⲡ *again*

ⲥⲱⲡ, ⲥⲡ-, ⲥⲟⲡ⸗ *dip, soak*

ⲥⲉⲉⲡⲉ [ⲥⲉⲡⲉⲓ] *remain;* m. *remainder, rest*
ⲁⲩⲱ ⲡⲕⲉⲥⲉⲉⲡⲉ *and so forth, et cetera*

ⲥⲡⲓⲣ m. *rib, side*

ⲥⲟⲡⲥⲡ [ⲥⲁⲡⲥⲡ], ⲥⲡⲥⲡ-, ⲥⲡⲥⲱⲡ⸗, ⲥⲉⲡⲥⲱⲡ† *often abbreviated* ⲥⲟⲡⲥ
[ⲥⲁⲡⲥ], ⲥⲡⲥ-, ⲥⲉⲡⲥ- *ask, beg, comfort;* m. *petition, encouragement*

ⲥⲡⲟⲧⲟⲩ m. *lips, shore*

ⲥⲓⲣ, ⲥⲁⲉⲓⲣ, ⲥⲁⲉⲓⲣⲉ m. *milk, butter, leaven*

ⲥⲱⲣ, ⲥⲣ̄-, ⲥⲟⲣ⸗, ⲥⲏⲣ† *spread, distribute;* m. *distribution*

ⲥⲟⲩⲣⲉ, ⲥⲉⲣ-, ⲥⲣ̄- f. *thorn, needle*

ⲥⲱⲣⲙ̄ [ⲥⲱⲣⲙⲉ], ⲥⲉⲣⲙ-, ⲥⲟⲣⲙ⸗, ⲥⲟⲣⲙ̄† [ⲥⲁⲣⲙ̄†] *get lost, stray, err, lead
astray;* m. *error*

ⲥⲣⲓⲧ, ⲥⲣⲁⲧ⸗ *glean, gather*

ⲥⲟⲣⲧ m.f. *wool*

ⲥⲣ̄ϥⲉ, ⲥⲣⲟϥⲧ† [ⲥⲣⲁⲃⲧ†] *be at leisure, unoccupied*

ⲥⲣⲟϥⲣϥ *fall, wither*
ⲥⲣϥⲣⲓϥⲉ pl. *crumbs*

[ⲥⲣⲁϩ, ⲥⲧⲣⲁϩ n. *example*
ⲣ̄ⲥⲣⲁϩ *set as an example, put to shame*]

ⲥⲁⲧ m. *tail*

ⲥⲁⲁⲧ⸗ v. ⲥⲓⲛⲉ *pass by*

ⲥⲓⲧ m. *basilisk*

ⲥⲟⲉⲓⲧ m. *fame, report*

ⲥⲱⲧ [ⲥⲱⲧⲉ], ⲥⲟⲧ⸗ (ⲉ-) *return, repeat, also means, stretch, reach*

ⲥⲁⲧⲉ [ⲥⲉⲧⲉ] f. *fire*

ⲥⲓⲧⲉ, ⲥⲁⲧ⸗, ⲥⲉⲧ⸗, ⲥⲏⲧ† [ⲥⲁⲧⲉ†] *throw, sow*
ⲥⲟⲧⲉ [ⲥⲁⲧⲉ], pl. ⲥⲟⲟⲧⲉ m.f. *arrow*

ⲥⲟⲧⲉ [ⲉⲥⲟⲧⲉ] n. *measure*

ⲥⲱⲧⲉ, ⲥⲉⲧ-, ⲥⲟⲧ⸗, ⲥⲁⲧ⸗ *redeem, rescue, save;* [ⲥⲱⲧ] m. *ransom,
redemption*
ⲣⲉϥⲥⲱⲧⲉ m. *redeemer*

ⲥⲧⲟ, ⲥⲧⲉ-, ⲥⲧⲟ⸗ v. ⲧⲥⲧⲟ *bring back*

ⲥⲧⲟⲓ̈, ⲥⲧ̄- m. *smell, fragrant plant*
ⲥⲧ̄ⲛⲟⲩϥⲉ [ⲥⲧ̄ⲛⲟⲩⲃⲉ] m. *perfume, incense*
ⲥⲧ̄ⲃⲱⲱⲛ m. *stench*

ⲥⲱⲧⲙ̄, ⲥⲉⲧⲙ̄-, ⲥⲟⲧⲙ⸗ [ⲥⲁⲧⲙ⸗] (ⲉ-) *hear, listen to;* m. *hearing* ⲥⲱⲧⲙ̅ ⲛ̅- *obey*

ⲥⲱⲧⲙ̅ ⲛ̅ⲥⲁ-,ⲛ̅ⲥⲱⲥ *obey*

ⲁⲧⲥⲱⲧⲙ̅ *disobedient*

ⲥⲧⲙ̅ⲏⲧ *obedient* (ⲥⲉⲧⲙ̅ϩⲏⲧ)

ⲥⲱⲧⲡ,ⲥⲉⲧⲡ-,ⲥⲟⲧⲡⲥ,ⲥⲟⲧⲡ† [ⲥⲁⲧⲡ†,ⲥⲁⲧⲡⲉ†] *choose, be chosen†, better†;* m. *chosen, elect* person or thing

ⲥⲱⲧⲣ̅,ⲥⲟⲧⲣ̅† *be turned, twisted*

ⲥⲁⲧⲉⲉⲣⲉ f. *stater, coin* (στατήρ)

ⲥⲧⲱⲧ *tremble;* m. *trembling*

ⲥⲱⲧϥ,ⲥⲉⲧϥ-,ⲥⲟⲧϥⲥ,ⲥⲟⲧϥ† *be pure, clear, purify;* m. *purity*

ⲥⲧⲉⲓⲱϩⲉ,ⲥⲧⲱϩⲉ *acre* v. ⲉⲓⲱϩⲉ

ⲥⲏⲩ [ⲥⲏⲟⲩ],ⲥⲟⲩ- m. *time, season*

ⲛ̅ⲥⲟⲩⲁ,ⲛ̅ⲥⲟⲩⲟⲩⲁ *on the first day*

ⲥⲓⲟⲩ,ⲥⲟⲩ- m. *star*

ⲥⲟⲟⲩ [ⲥⲁⲩ], f. ⲥⲟ,ⲥⲟⲉ,ⲥⲉⲩ-,-ⲁⲥⲉ *six*

ⲥⲉ *sixty*

ⲥⲟⲩⲟ m. *wheat, grain*

ⲥⲟⲩⲉⲗⲟⲩⲱⲗⲥ,ⲥⲟⲩⲗⲱⲗ† *wrap up*

ⲥⲟⲟⲩⲛ̅ [ⲥⲟⲟⲩⲛⲉ,ⲥⲁⲩⲛⲉ],ⲥⲟⲩⲛ-,ⲥⲟⲩⲱⲛ-,ⲥⲟⲩⲱⲛⲥ *know;* m. *knowledge*

ⲣ̅-(oⲧ ⲛ̅-) ⲁⲧⲥⲟⲟⲩⲛ̅ *be ignorant*

ⲥⲟⲩⲛ̅ⲧⲥ m. *price, value of*

ⲥⲓⲟⲩⲣ m. *eunuch*

ⲥⲟⲩⲥⲟⲩ m. *moment, second*

ⲥⲟⲟⲩⲧⲛ̅ [ⲥⲁⲩⲧⲛ̅],ⲥⲟⲩⲧⲛ-,ⲥⲟⲩⲧⲱⲛⲥ,ⲥⲟⲩⲧⲱⲛ† *be straight, upright, set straight, stretch;* m. *uprightness*

ⲥⲱⲟⲩϩ,ⲥⲉⲩϩ-,ⲥⲟⲟⲩϩⲥ [ⲥⲁϩⲥ],ⲥⲟⲟⲩϩ† [ⲥⲁⲩϩ†,ⲥⲟϩⲟⲩ†] *be gathered, gather, collect, be assembled†*

ⲥⲱⲟⲩϩ ⲉϩⲟⲩⲛ *gather together*

ⲥⲟⲟⲩϩⲥ [ⲥⲁⲟⲩϩⲥ] f. *congregation, gathering*

ⲥⲟⲟⲩϩⲉ f. *egg*

ⲥⲟⲉⲓϣ [ⲥⲁⲉⲓϣ] m. *pair, couple, [mate]*

ⲥⲱϣ,ⲥⲉϣ-,ϣⲉⲥ-,ⲥⲟϣⲥ *strike, hit*

ⲥⲁϣ, pl. ⲥⲏϣⲉ,ⲥϣ-,ϣⲥ-,ϣⲉ- m.f. *stroke, blow, sore, wound*

ⲥⲱϣ,ϣⲱⲥ,ⲥⲟϣⲥ [ⲥⲁϣⲥ],ϣⲟⲥⲥ,ⲥⲏϣ†,ϣⲏⲥ† *despise, insult, be humbled;* m. *shame, contempt*

ⲥⲱϣϥ,ⲥⲟϣϥ† *means the same*

ⲥϣⲉ v. ϣϣⲉ *be suitable*

ⲥⲓϣⲉ,ⲥⲁϣⲉ† *be bitter;* m. *bitterness, gall*

ⲥⲱϣⲉ f. *field, country*

ⲥⲱϣⲙ̅,ϣⲱⲥⲙ̅,ⲥⲟϣⲙ̅†,ϣⲟⲥⲙ̅† *be faint, disheartened*

ⲥⲱϣⲙ̅ ⲉ- *annoy*

ⲥⲁϣⲧ† v. ⲥⲱϩⲉ *weave*

ⲥⲱϣⲧ,ⲥⲉϣⲧ-,ⲥⲟϣⲧⲥ [ϣⲉϣⲧⲥ],ⲥⲟϣⲧ†,ⲥⲁϣⲧ† *stop, obstruct, keep from*

ϣⲟϣⲧ [ϣⲁϣⲧ] m. *key*

ⲥⲁϣϥ [ⲥⲟϣϥ,ⲥⲟϣϥⲉ], f. ⲥⲁϣϥⲉ,-ⲥⲁϣϥⲉ *seven*

ⲙⲉϩⲥⲁϣϥ *seventh*

ϣϥⲉ,ϣⲃⲉ *seventy*

ⲥⲁϥ,ⲛ̅ⲥⲁϥ m. *yesterday*

cⲱⲱϥ [cⲱϥ], cⲉⲉϥ-, cⲉⲉⲃⲉ-, cooϥ⸗, cooⲃ⸗, cooϥᵗ   *be defiled, defile, dirty, pollute;* m. *pollution, abomination*

cⲏϥⲉ, cⲏⲃⲉ   f. *sword, knife*

coϥⲧⲉ v. coⲃⲧⲉ   *prepare;* m. *equipment*

ciⲍⲉ, cⲉⲍ-, cⲁⲍⲧ⸗, cⲉⲍⲧ⸗   *be removed, move, withdraw*

cooⲍⲉ, coⲍⲉ, cⲁⲍⲉ-, cⲁⲍⲱ⸗ [cⲉⲍⲱ⸗], cⲁⲍⲏⲩᵗ (ⲉⲃoⲗ)   *remove, withdraw oneself (from)*

cooⲍⲉ, coⲍⲉ, cⲁⲍⲉ-, cⲁⲍⲱ⸗ [cⲉⲍⲱ⸗]   *set upright* (caus. of ⲱⲍⲉ)
    cooⲍⲉ, coⲍⲉ, [cⲱⲍⲉ]   *reprimand, scold;* m. *disapproval*

cⲱⲍⲉ, cⲁⲍⲧ-, cⲁⲍⲧ⸗, cⲁⲍⲧᵗ, cⲁⲱⲧᵗ   *weave*

cⲍⲁⲓ [cⲍⲉⲉi], cⲍⲁⲓ̈-, cⲉⲍ⸗, cⲁⲍ⸗, cⲍⲁⲓ̈c⸗, cⲁⲍⲧ⸗, cⲉⲍⲧ⸗ [cⲍⲏⲧ⸗], cⲏⲍᵗ
    [cⲍⲏoⲩⲧᵗ]   *write, be written*ᵗ, *scripture*ᵗ; [pl. cⲍⲉⲉi] m. *writing, letter*
    cⲁⲍ   m.f. *teacher, master*

cⲍⲃⲏⲏⲧⲉ, cⲃⲏⲏⲧⲉ, ⲍⲃⲏⲧⲉ   m. *foam*

cⲍⲓⲙⲉ, pl. ⲍioⲙⲉ [ⲍiⲁⲙⲉ, cⲍioⲙⲉ]   f. *woman, female*
    ϫicⲍiⲙⲉ   *marry*
    [ⲘⲚⲧcⲍiⲙⲉ   f. *femaleness, womanliness, womankind*]

cⲁⲍⲛⲉ   *provide, supply;* m. *provision*
    oⲩⲉⲍcⲁⲍⲛⲉ [oⲩⲁⲍcⲁⲍⲛⲉ]   *command, place an order*

cⲱⲍⲡ, cⲉⲍⲡ-, cⲁⲍⲡ⸗   *suck, drink*

cⲱⲍⲣ̄, cⲉⲍⲣ-, cⲁⲍⲣ⸗, cⲁⲍⲣ̄ᵗ   *sweep*

cⲁⲍcⲍ, cⲉⲍcⲱⲍ⸗   *roll up*

cⲁⲍoⲩ, cⲁⲍoⲩⲉ [coⲩⲍⲱⲣ], cⲍoⲩⲣ-, cⲍoⲩⲱⲣ⸗, cⲍoⲩoⲣⲧᵗ   *curse;* m. *curse*

[cⲱϫⲉ] v. ϣⲱϫⲉ   *wrestle*

[cⲁϫⲛⲉ] v. ϣoϫⲛⲉ   *take counsel*

[cⲱϫⲡ] v. ϣⲱϫⲡ   *remain over*

cⲏϭ   f. *foal, colt*

coϭ [cⲉϭⲉ]   m. *fool, foolish, silly*

cⲱϭ, cⲉϭ-, coϭ⸗, cⲏϭᵗ   *be paralyzed*

coϭⲛ̄   m. *ointment*

cϭⲏⲣ   *sail;* m. *voyage*

cϭⲣⲁⲍⲧᵗ, cϭⲣⲉⲍⲧᵗ   *rest*ᵗ, *pause*ᵗ; m. *quiet, tranquility*

Ⲧ

called ⲧⲁⲩ   transliterated *t*

Ⲧ̄   as number *three hundred*

ⲧ   sometimes replaces ⲇ, ⲕ and ϭ

ⲧ-, ⲧⲉ-   def. article sing. fem. *the* v. ⲡ-

-ⲧ   suffix pronoun 1st person sing. after consonants *me* v. -ï

ⲧⲁ-, ⲧⲉ⸗   possessive *that which belongs to, of* v. ⲡⲁ- and ⲡⲉ⸗

ⲧⲁ-   (for Ⲛ̄ⲧⲁ-) conjunctive 1st person sing.

ⲧⲁï   *here*

ⲧⲁï, ⲧⲉï-   *this* sing. fem. v. ⲡⲁï

ⲧⲁïo, ⲧⲁⲉiⲉ-, ⲧⲁⲉio⸗ [ⲧⲁⲉiⲁ⸗], ⲧⲁⲉiⲏⲩᵗ [ⲧⲁⲉiⲏoⲩⲧᵗ, ⲧⲁⲉiⲁⲉiⲧᵗ]   *honor;*
    m. *honor, gift*

ⲧⲉ-   personal pronoun 2nd person sing. fem. *you*

ⲧⲉ   copular pronoun f. *she is, it is* v. ⲡⲉ

ⲧⲏ, ⲧⲉ m. *time, season*

ⲧⲏ demonstrative pronoun f. *that* v. ⲡⲏ

　　ϯ- demonstrative article f. v. ⲡⲓ-

ϯ- personal pronoun 1st person sing. *I*

ϯ, ϯ-, ⲧⲁⲁ⳨ [ⲧⲉⲉ⳨, ⲧⲉⲉⲓⲧ⳨], ⲧⲟⲧ, ⲧⲱⲧ [ⲧⲉⲧ, ⲧⲟⲉⲧ, ⲧⲟⲉⲓⲧ, ⲧⲟⲉⲓⲉⲧ,
　　ⲧⲱⲉⲓⲧ], p.c. ⲧⲁⲓ- *give*; m. *gift*
　　imper. ⲙⲁ, ⲙⲏⲉⲓ⳨, ⲙⲁϯ
　　ⲧⲛ̄ with dative ⲛⲁ⳨
　　ϯ ⲛ̄ⲥⲁ-, ⲛ̄ⲥⲱ⳨ *pursue*
　　ϯ ϩⲓ-, ϩⲓⲱⲱ⳨ *clothe, put on, wear*
　　ⲥⲧⲟⲧ *it is fitting*
　　ϯ ⲉⲃⲟⲗ *sell*
　　ϯ ⲙⲛ̄- *fight with*
　　ϯ ⲟⲩⲃⲉ- *fight against*
　　ϯ plus noun forms many compound verbs v. ⲉⲟⲟⲩ, ⲣⲁⲛ, ϩⲏⲩ, and others
　　[ϯⲏ n. *emanation*]

ϯⲉ, ϯ, -ⲧⲏ v. ϯⲟⲩ *five*

ⲧⲟ m. *land, earth*

ⲧⲟⲉ, ⲧⲟ [ⲧⲁⲉⲓⲉ] f. *part, share*
　　ⲙⲁⲓ̈ⲧⲟ ⲛ̄ϩⲟⲩⲟ *covetous* (ⲙⲉ *love*)

ⲧⲱ⳨ possessive pronoun f. *that which belongs to* v. ⲡⲱ⳨

ⲧⲏⲏⲃⲉ, ⲧⲏⲃⲉ, ⲧⲉⲃⲉ m. *finger, toe*

ⲧⲱⲃⲉ name of 5th Egyptian month

ⲧⲱⲱⲃⲉ, ⲧⲱⲃⲉ f. *brick* (hence adobe)

ⲧⲱⲱⲃⲉ, ⲧⲟⲟⲃ⳨, ⲧⲟⲟⲃⲉⲧ *seal, stamp*; m. *seal*

ⲧⲱⲱⲃⲉ, ⲧⲟⲟⲃ⳨ *repay*; m. *repayment*

ⲧⲃⲁ *ten thousand, myriad*

ⲧⲃ̄ⲃⲟ [ⲧⲟⲩⲃⲟ], ⲧⲃ̄ⲃⲉ-, ⲧⲃ̄ⲃⲟ⳨ [ⲧⲟⲩⲃⲁ⳨], ⲧⲃ̄ⲃⲏⲩⲧ [ⲧⲟⲩⲃⲏⲩⲧ,
　　ⲧⲟⲩⲃⲏⲟⲩⲧ, ⲧⲟⲩⲃⲁⲉⲓⲧ] *cleanse, purify* (caus. of ⲟⲩⲟⲡ);
　　m. *purification, purity*

ⲧⲃ̄ⲛⲏ, pl. ⲧⲃ̄ⲛⲟⲟⲩⲉ m. *farm animal: cow, donkey*, etc.

ⲧⲃⲏⲣ m. *kick*

ϯⲃⲥ m. *heel*

ⲧⲱ̄ⲃⲥ, ⲧⲃⲥ-, ⲧⲟⲃⲥ⳨ *goad, incite, prod*

ⲧⲃ̄ⲧ, ⲧⲏⲃⲧ m. *fish*

ⲧⲟⲃⲧⲃ̄, ⲧⲃ̄ⲧⲱⲃ⳨ *form, invent*

ⲧⲱⲃϩ, ⲧⲃϩ-, ⲧⲟⲃϩ⳨ *pray, ask*; m. *prayer*

ⲧⲉⲕ-, ⲧⲟⲟⲕ⳨ v. ⲧⲱⲱϭⲉ *be joined*

ⲧⲱⲕ, ⲧⲟⲕ⳨, ⲧⲏⲕⲧ *be strong, strengthen*
　　[ⲧⲱⲕ ⲁⲣⲉⲧ⳨ *establish, be firm*]
　　ⲧⲱⲕ ⲉϩⲟⲩⲛ *persist*
　　ⲧⲱⲕ ⲛ̄ϩⲏⲧ *show courage*

ⲧⲱⲕ, ⲧⲱϭ, ⲧⲟⲕ⳨, ⲧⲁⲕ⳨, ⲧⲟϭ⳨ *heat, kindle*
　　ⲓⲛⲧⲱⲕ, ⲛ̄ⲧⲱⲕ m. *oven, furnace*
　　ⲧⲱϭ *bake*
　　ϯⲕ m. *spark*

ⲧⲁⲕⲟ [ⲧⲉⲕⲟ], ⲧⲁⲕⲉ-, ⲧⲁⲕⲟ⳨ [ⲧⲉⲕⲁ⳨], ⲧⲁⲕⲏⲩⲧ *destroy, perish, be
　　corrupt*; m. *ruin*
　　ⲙⲛ̄ⲧⲁⲧⲧⲁⲕⲟ f. *incorruption, imperishability*

ⲦⲰⲔⲘ̄, ⲦⲈⲔⲘ-, ⲦⲞⲔⲘⳇ, ⲦⲀⲔⲘ̄† *pluck, pull, drag*

ⲦⲰⲔⳞ, ⲦⲈⲔⳞ-, ⲦⲞⳔⳇ, ⲦⲞⲔⳚ† *be pierced, stuck, pierce, goad*

ⲦⲔⲀⳚ, ⲔⲀⳚ m. *pain*

[ⲦⲔⲀⲦⲞ, ⲦⲔⲦⲞ] ⲔⲦⲞ, [ⲦⲔⲦⲈ-] ⲔⲦⲈ-, [ⲦⲔⲦⲞⳇ, ⲔⲞⲦⳇ]ⲔⲦⲞⳇ, ⲔⲦⲎⲨ†,
  ⲔⲦⲀⲈⲓⲦ† *turn, return, go around, surround, be turned*† (caus. of ⲔⲰⲦⲈ)

ⲦⲀⲖⲞ [ⲦⲈⲖⲞ], ⲦⲀⲖⲈ-, ⲦⲀⲖⲞⳇ, ⲦⲀⲖⲎⲨ†, ⲦⲀⲖⲈ† *lift up, offer up, go up,*
  mount, be seated†; m. *raising up, offering*
    ⲦⲀⲖⲞ ⲈⳘⲢⲀ̈ⲓ *raise*

ⲦⲰⲖⲔ, ⲦⲞⲖⲔⳇ *pluck out*

ⲦⲈⲖⲎⲖ [† ⲀⲖⲎⲖ] *rejoice*; m. *joy*

ⲦⲰⲖⲘ̄, ⲦⲞⲖⳇ, ⲦⲞⲖⳞ† *be dirty, defile*; m. *stain, pollution*

ⲦⲖⲞⳘ, ⲦⲚⲞⳘ, pl. ⲦⲖⲞⲞⳘ, ⲦⲚⲞⲞⳘ m. *furrow*

Ⲧⲗ̄Ⲧⲗ̄ *drip*
    Ⲧⲗ̄ⲦⲗⲈ f. *drop*

ⲦⲀⲖⳠⲞ [Ⲧⲗ̄ⳠⲞ], ⲦⲀⲖⳠⲈ-, ⲦⲀⲖⳠⲞⳇ [Ⲧⲗ̄ⳠⲀⳇ], ⲦⲀⲖⳠⲎⲨ† *heal, cure*;
  m. *healing*

ⲦⲘ̄- negates infinitive, conjunctive, causative, conditional, and temporal
  conjugations

ⲦⲰⳘ, ⲦⳘ̄-, ⲦⲞⳘⳇ, ⲦⲎⳘⳇ† *shut, close*
    ⲦⳘ̄Ⲣⲱⳇ *be silent*
    ⲦⲰⳘ ⲚⳘⳌⲎⲦ m. *hardness of heart*

ⲦⲰⳘ, ⲦⲎⳘ† *sharpen, be sharp*†

ⲦⲀⳘⲓⲞ, ⲦⲀⳘⲓⲈ-, ⲦⲀⳘⲓⲞⳇ, ⲦⲀⳘⲓⲎⲨ† *make, create*; m. *creation, creature*

ⲦⲀⳘⲞ, ⲦⲀⳘⲈ-, ⲦⲀⳘⲞⳇ [ⲦⲀⳘⲀⳇ, ⲦⲀⳘⲀⲈⲓⲦ†] *tell, explain, inform* (caus. of
  ⲈⲓⳘⲈ)
    [ⲢⲈ̄ⲨⲦⲀⳘⲞ m.f. *instructor*]

†ⳘⲈ, ⲦⲓⳘⲈ, pl. ⲦⳘⲈ m. *village, town*
    ⲢⳘⲚ̄†ⳘⲈ n. *villager, citizen*

ⲦⲰⲰⳘⲈ, ⲦⲞⳘⲈ† [ⲦⲀⳘⲈ†] *join, be fitting*†; m. *union*

ⲦⳘⲀⲓ̈Ⲟ, ⲦⳘⲀⲓ̈Ⲉ-, ⲦⳘⲀⲓ̈Ⲟⳇ, ⲦⳘⲀⲓ̈ⲎⲨ† *justify, praise*; m. *justification*

ⲦⳘⲎ f. *mat*

ⲦⳘ̄ⳘⲞ, ⲦⳘⲈ-, ⲦⳘⲞⳇ, ⲦⳘ̄ⳘⲎⲨ† *feed, nourish* (caus. of ⲞⲨⲰⳘ)

ⲦⲰⳘⳚ, ⲦⳘ̄Ⳛ-, ⲦⲞⳘⳚⳇ, ⲦⲞⳘⳚ† *bury*

ⲦⲰⳘⲦ, ⲦⲰⳘⲚ̄Ⲧ (Ⲉ-) *meet, happen upon, encounter*

ⲦⳘ̄ⳌⲞ, ⲦⳘ̄ⳌⲈ-, ⲦⳘ̄ⳌⲞⳇ *set on fire*; m. *burning*

ⲦⲚ̄- personal pronoun 1st person pl. *we*

-ⲦⲚ̄ suffix pronoun 2nd person pl. *you*

ⲦⲚ̄-, ⲦⲞⲞⲦⳇ v. ⲦⲰⲢⲈ *hand*

ⲦⲰⲚ [ⲦⲞ, ⲦⲞⲚ] *where?, from where?, how?*
    ⲈⲦⲰⲚ *to what place?*
    Ⲛ̄ⲦⲰⲚ *where?*
    ⲈⲂⲞⲖ ⲦⲰⲚ *from where?*

ⲦⲰⲚ in †ⲦⲰⲚ *fight, argue*; m. *argument, quarrel*

ⲦⲰⲰⲚ v. ⲦⲰⲞⲨⲚ̄ *arise*

ⲦⲀⲚⲞ [ⲦⲈⲚⲞ, ⲦⲈⲚⲈ-], ⲦⲀⲚⲞⳇ *make, produce*

ⲦⲎⲚⲈ m. *dam, dike*

[ⲦⲎⲚⲈ] v. ⲦⲎⲨⲦⲚ̄ *you* pl.

ⲦⲰⲚⲞⲨ, ⲦⲞⲚⲱ *very, greatly*
    ⳚⲈ ⲦⲰⲚⲞⲨ *yes indeed*

ⲦⲚⲞⲘ v. ⲦⲀⲞⲘ *furrow*

ⲦⲚ̄ⲚⲞ [ⲦⲀⲚⲞ], ⲦⲚ̄ⲚⲞⲠ, ⲦⲚ̄ⲞⲠ, ⲦⲚ̄ⲚⲎⲨ† [ⲦⲚ̄ⲚⲞⲈⲒⲦ†] *pound, trample*
  ⲐⲚ̄Ⲟ, ⲐⲚ̄ⲞⲠ, ⲐⲚ̄ⲚⲎⲨ† *crush*

ⲦⲚ̄ⲚⲞⲞⲨ [ⲦⲚ̄ⲚⲀⲨ], ⲦⲚ̄ⲚⲈⲨ-, ⲦⲚ̄ⲚⲞⲞⲨⲠ *send* (caus. of ⲈⲒⲚⲈ)

ⲦⲞⲚⲦⲚ̄ [ⲦⲀⲚⲦⲚ̄], ⲦⲚ̄ⲦⲚ-, ⲦⲚ̄ⲦⲰⲚⲠ, ⲦⲚ̄ⲦⲰⲚ† [ⲦⲚ̄ⲦⲀⲚⲦ†] *be like,*
  compare, make a comparison; m. *likeness*

ⲦⲈⲚⲞⲨ, †ⲚⲞⲨ *now* v. ⲞⲨⲚⲞⲨ

ⲦⲚⲀⲨ *when?* v. ⲚⲀⲨ

ⲦⲚ̄Ⲅ m. *wing*

ⲦⲀⲚⲠⲞ [ⲦⲚ̄Ⲅ̄Ⲟ], ⲦⲀⲚⲠⲞⲠ *make alive, be alive* (caus. of ⲰⲚⲅ̄)

ⲦⲀⲚⲅⲞⲨⲦ, ⲦⲀⲚⲅⲞⲨⲦⲠ [ⲦⲚ̄ⲅⲞⲨⲦⲠ], ⲦⲀⲚⲅⲎⲨⲦ† *trust, believe*

ⲦⲀⲠ m. *horn*

ⲦⲞⲠ [ⲦⲀⲠ] m. *edge, end, border, bosom*

ⲦⲰⲠ *stitch*
  ⲅⲀⲘⲚ̄ⲦⲰⲠ m. *needle*

ⲦⲰⲠ, ⲦⲰⲰⲠ, ⲦⲈⲠ-, ⲦⲞⲠⲠ, ⲦⲎⲠ† *be accustomed, familiar;* m. *custom*

ⲦⲠⲈ m. *upper part*
  Ⲛ̄ⲦⲠⲈ *above, over, up*
  ⲤⲀⲚ̄ⲦⲠⲈ *above*
  Ⲣ̄ⲦⲠⲈ *surmount*

†ⲠⲈ f. *loins*

ⲦⲰⲠⲈ, ⲦⲰⲠ-, ⲦⲞⲠⲠ *taste*
  †ⲠⲈ f. *taste*
  ⲬⲒ†ⲠⲈ *taste*

ⲦⲀⲠⲚ̄ m. *cumin*

ⲦⲀⲠⲢⲞ f. *mouth* (literally and figuratively)

ⲦⲀⲢ m. *branch*

ⲦⲎⲢⲠ *all, whole, every*
  ⲠⲦⲎⲢϥ *all things, everything, creation, the universe* [*the All, the Entirety* of
  divine attributes or beings]
  ⲈⲠⲦⲎⲢϥ *at all*

ⲦⲀⲢⲈⲠ, ⲦⲀⲢⲈ- conjugation base future conjunctive

ⲦⲰⲢⲈ, ⲦⲞⲞⲦⲠ f. *hand* (only in compounds, cf. ϬⲒⲬ)
  ⲦⲞⲦ- with ⲦⲎⲨⲦⲚ̄ [ⲦⲎⲚⲈ]
  ⲈⲒⲢⲈ Ⲛ̄ⲀⲦⲞⲞⲦⲠ, Ⲣ̄ⲀⲠⲀⲦⲞⲞⲦⲠ *endeavor, try*
  ⲔⲰ Ⲛ̄ⲦⲞⲞⲦⲠ ⲈⲂⲞⲖ, ⲔⲀⲦⲞⲞⲦⲠ ⲈⲂⲞⲖ *cease, despair*
  † Ⲛ̄ⲦⲞⲞⲦⲠ *help*
  ϢⲈⲠⲦⲞⲞⲦⲠ *grasp the hand of*
  ϢⲠ̄ⲦⲰⲢⲈ, ϢⲦⲰⲢⲈ *guarantee*
  forming prepositions:
  ⲈⲦⲚ̄-, ⲈⲦⲞⲞⲦⲠ *to*
  Ⲛ̄ⲦⲚ̄-, Ⲛ̄ⲦⲞⲞⲦⲠ *in, by, with, beside, from, through, because of, to*
  ⲅⲀⲦⲚ̄-, ⲅⲀⲦⲞⲞⲦⲠ *with, beside, at*
  ⲅⲒⲦⲚ̄-, ⲅⲒⲦⲞⲞⲦⲠ *through, by, from, by means of*
  ⲈⲂⲞⲖ ⲅⲒⲦⲚ̄-, ⲈⲂⲞⲖ ⲅⲒⲦⲞⲞⲦⲠ *through, by, from, by means of*

ⲦⲢⲀ f. *joint*

ⲦⲢⲈⲠ, ⲦⲢⲈ- causative infinitive, often translates as *that*
  actually a verb *cause to do,* itself taking a
  conjugation base or the coordinating Ⲉ-

ϩⲙ̄ⲡⲧⲣⲉ⸗ *while, as, when, by*
ⲙⲁⲣⲉ⸗, ⲙⲁⲣⲉ- q.v., causative imper. *may, let*
ⲧⲁⲣⲕⲟ, ⲧⲁⲣⲕⲉ-, ⲧⲁⲣⲕⲟ⸗ *make to swear, adjure* (caus. of ⲱⲣⲕ)
ⲧⲣⲱⲙ m. *storm, hurricane*
ⲧⲱⲣⲡ, ⲧⲟⲣⲡ⸗ *seize, rob, carry off;* m. *plunder*
ⲧⲱⲣⲡ, ⲧⲟⲣⲡ⸗, ⲧⲟⲣⲡ† *sew, stitch*
ⲧⲣⲓⲣ f. *oven*
ⲧⲣ̄ⲣⲉ [ⲧⲣ̄ⲣⲓⲉ], ⲧⲣ̄ⲉⲓⲱⲟⲩ† *be afraid, frightened*
ⲧⲱⲣⲧ m. *staircase*
ⲧⲱⲣⲧⲣ̄ m. *step, degree*
ⲧⲱⲣϣ *be red, blush*
ⲧⲣⲟϣ, ⲧⲟⲣϣ† means the same
ⲧⲣⲟϣⲣⲉϣ, ⲧⲣⲉϣⲣⲱϣ† means the same
ⲧⲱⲣϩ, ⲧⲟⲣϩ† *be sober*
ⲧⲟⲉⲓⲥ f. *rag, patch*
ⲧⲱⲥ, ⲧⲉⲥ-, ⲧⲟⲥ⸗, ⲧⲏⲥ† *be hard, stiff, fix*
ⲧⲥⲁⲉⲓⲟ [ⲧⲥⲁⲉⲓⲱ], ⲧⲥⲁⲉⲓⲟ⸗, ⲧⲥⲁⲓⲏⲩ† [ⲧⲥⲁⲉⲓⲁⲉⲓⲧ†] *make beautiful, decorate*
ⲧⲥⲓⲟ, ⲧⲥⲓⲟ⸗, ⲧⲥⲓⲏⲩ† *satisfy*
ⲧⲥⲟ, ⲧⲥⲟ⸗ *give to drink* (caus. of ⲥⲱ)
ⲧⲥⲁⲃⲟ [ⲧⲥⲉⲃⲟ], ⲧⲥⲁⲃⲉ- [ⲧⲥⲉⲃⲉ-], ⲧⲥⲁⲃⲟ⸗ [ⲧⲥⲉⲃⲁ⸗, ⲧⲥⲉⲃⲟ⸗], ⲧⲥⲁⲃⲏⲩ† *teach, show* (caus. of ⲥⲁⲃⲉ); m. *teaching, instruction*
ⲥⲃⲟ [ⲥⲉⲃⲟ], ⲥⲃⲱ *learn*
ⲧⲥⲃ̄ⲕⲟ, ⲧⲥⲃ̄ⲕⲟ⸗ [ⲧⲥⲃ̄ⲕⲁ⸗], ⲧⲥⲃ̄ⲕⲏⲩ† *reduce, diminish*
ⲧⲥⲁⲛⲟ [ⲧⲥⲉⲛⲟ], ⲧⲥⲁⲛⲟ⸗ [ⲧⲥⲉⲛⲁ⸗], ⲧⲥⲁⲛⲏⲩ† *adorn, decorate, set in order*
ⲧⲥⲛ̄ⲕⲟ *breast-feed, nurse*
ⲧⲥⲧⲟ, ⲧⲥⲧⲉ-, ⲧⲥⲧⲟ⸗ [ⲧⲥⲧⲁ⸗], ⲧⲥⲧⲏⲩ† also written ⲥⲧⲟ, ⲥⲧⲉ-, ⲥⲧⲟ⸗ [ⲥⲧⲁ⸗], ⲥⲧⲏⲩ† *bring back, pay back, repeat, return* (caus. of ⲥⲱⲧ)
ⲧⲥⲧⲟ ⲉⲃⲟⲗ *turn out, reject, return*
ⲧⲟⲉⲓⲧ *mourn;* m. *lament, dirge*
ⲧⲟⲟⲧ⸗ v. ⲧⲱⲣⲉ *hand*
ⲧⲱⲧ, ⲧⲉⲧ-, ⲧⲟⲧ⸗ [ⲧⲁⲧ⸗], ⲧⲏⲧ† *be joined, be persuaded, agree, mingle;* m. *agreement*
ⲧⲱⲧ ⲛ̄ϩⲏⲧ *satisfy, consent, agree*
ⲧⲁⲁⲧⲉ, ⲧⲟⲟⲧⲉ, ⲧⲁⲁⲧⲉ†, ⲧⲟⲟⲧⲉ† *shine*
ⲧⲟⲧⲉ [ⲧⲉⲧⲉ] v. ⲟⲟⲧⲉ *womb*
ⲧⲱⲧⲉ f. *hem, fringe*
(ⲧⲧⲟ), ⲧⲧⲉ-, ⲧⲉ-, ⲧⲧⲟ⸗, ⲧⲟ⸗ *make give, require* (caus. of ϯ) imper. ⲙⲁⲧ⸗
ⲧⲉⲧⲛ̄- personal pronoun 2nd person pl. *you*
ⲧⲏⲩ, ⲧⲏⲟⲩ, ⲧⲟⲩ- m. *wind*
ⲧⲟⲩⲣⲏⲥ *south wind*
ϩⲁⲧⲏⲟⲩ f. *whirlwind, stormwind*
ϯⲟⲩ, f. ϯⲉ, ϯ, -ⲧⲏ *five*
ⲧⲁⲓ̈ⲟⲩ *fifty*
ⲧⲟⲟⲩ [ⲧⲁⲩ], pl. ⲧⲟⲩⲉⲓⲏ m. *mountain, monastic community*
ⲧⲟⲟⲩ, ⲧⲉⲩ-, ⲧⲟⲟⲩ⸗ *buy, purchase*
ⲧⲁⲟⲩⲟ, ⲧⲁⲟⲩⲱ [ⲧⲉⲟⲩⲟ, ⲧⲉⲩⲟ], ⲧⲁⲩⲉ- [ⲧⲉⲩⲉ-], ⲧⲁⲩⲟ⸗ *send, produce,*

proclaim, recite, name

ⲦⲞⲞⲨⲈ   m. *sandal, sandals*

ⲦⲞⲨⲞ, ⲦⲞⲨⲞ⸗   *show, teach*

ⲦⲞⲨⲈⲒⲞ [ⲦⲞⲨⲈⲒⲈ-]   *repay, return;* m. *repayment*

ⲦⲞⲨⲰ⸗   n. *bosom of, breast of*

     ⲈⲦⲞⲨⲚ-, ⲈⲦⲞⲨⲰ⸗   *beside, at, with*

     ϨⲒⲦⲞⲨⲚ-, ϨⲒⲦⲞⲨⲰ⸗   *beside, next*

     ⲠⲈⲦϨⲒⲦⲞⲨⲰ⸗   *neighbor*

ⲦⲰⲞⲨⲚ, ⲦⲰⲰⲚ [ⲦⲰⲞⲨⲚⲞⲨ], ⲦⲞⲨⲚ-, ⲦⲰⲞⲨⲚ⸗, ⲦⲰⲚ⸗   *arise, raise;*
     m. *resurrection*

     ⲦⲰⲞⲨⲚ ϨⲀ-   *bear*

ⲦⲞⲨⲚⲞⲤ, ⲦⲞⲨⲚⲈⲤ-, ⲦⲞⲨⲚⲞⲤ⸗ [ⲦⲞⲨⲚⲀⲤ⸗]   *wake, raise, set up* (caus. of
     ⲞⲨⲰⲚ)

     ⲦⲞⲨⲚⲈⲒⲀⲦ⸗   *instruct* v. ⲈⲒⲀ

ⲦⲞⲨⲰⲦ, [pl. ⲦⲞⲨⲞⲦⲈ]   f. *idol, shrine*

ⲦⲞⲞⲨⲦⲈ, ⲦⲞⲨⲎⲦ†   *be gathered, collected, gather*

ⲐⲨⲦⲚ̄ [ⲐⲞⲨⲦⲚ̄, ⲐⲎⲚⲈ]   pronoun 2nd person pl. *you*

ⲦⲞⲨϪⲞ, ⲦⲞⲨϪⲈ-, ⲦⲞⲨϪⲞ⸗ [ⲦⲞⲨϪⲀ⸗], ⲦⲞⲨϪⲎⲨ† [ⲦⲞⲨϪⲞⲈⲒⲦ†]   *save,*
     heal, be saved, be safe† (caus. of ⲞⲨϪⲀⲓ)

ⲦⲰϢ [ⲦⲰϢⲈ], ⲦⲈϢ-, ⲦⲞϢ⸗ [ⲦⲀϢ⸗], ⲦⲎϢ†   *limit, determine, decide, fix,*
     be fixed; m. *ordinance, destiny*

     ⲦⲞϢ   m. *border, limit, district, nome*

     ⲦⲈϢⲈ   f. *neighbor*

ⲦⲀϢⲈ- (caus. of ⲰϢ) in ⲦⲀϢⲈⲞⲈⲒϢ   *proclaim, preach*

ⲦⲀϢⲞ, ⲦⲀϢⲈ-, ⲦⲀϢⲞ⸗   *increase* (caus. of ⲀϢⲀⲓ)

ⲦⲀϥ [ⲦⲎϥ]   m. *saliva*

ⲐⲈ   v. ϨⲈ   *manner*

ⲦⲰϨ   m. *chaff*

ⲦⲰϨ, ⲦⲈϨ-, ⲦⲀϨ⸗, ⲦⲎϨ†   *be mixed, be disturbed, mix, stir;* m. *mixture,*
     disturbance

ⲦⲀϨⲞ [ⲦⲈϨⲞ], ⲦⲀϨⲈ-, ⲦⲀϨⲞ⸗ [ⲦⲈϨⲀ⸗, ⲦⲈϨⲞ⸗], ⲦⲀϨⲎⲨ†   *set up, reach,*
     catch up, attain (caus. of ⲰϨⲈ)

     ⲀⲦⲦⲀϨⲞ⸗   *unattainable, incomprehensible*

     ⲦⲀϨⲞ ⲈⲢⲀⲦ⸗   *establish*

†ϨⲈ, ⲦⲀϨⲈ† [ⲦⲞϨⲈ†]   *get drunk;* m. *drunkenness*

ⲦϨⲒⲞ, ⲐⲒⲞ⸗   *cause to fall, bring down* (caus. of ϨⲈ)

ⲦϨⲞ, ⲐⲞ   *become bad;* m. *badness*

     ⲦϨⲞ Ⲉ-   *be worse than*

ⲐⲀⲂ   m. *leaven*

ⲐⲂⲂⲒⲞ [ⲐⲂⲈⲒⲞ], ⲐⲂ̄ⲂⲒⲈ-, ⲐⲂ̄ⲂⲒⲞ⸗ [ⲐⲂⲂⲒⲀ⸗], ⲐⲂ̄ⲂⲒⲎⲨ†, [ⲐⲂ̄ⲒⲎⲨ†, ⲐⲂ̄ⲂⲒⲀⲈⲒⲦ†,
     ⲐⲈⲂⲒⲎⲞⲨⲦ†]   *humiliate, be humble* (caus. of ϨⲂ̄ⲂⲈ); m. *humility*

ⲐⲎⲂⲀⲒⲤ   *the Thebaid,* the country around Thebes in Upper Egypt

ⲐⲀⲞ, ⲐⲀⲞ⸗   *make fly, drive away, scatter*

ⲦⲰϨⲘ̄ [ⲦⲰϨⲘⲈ], ⲦⲈϨⲘ-, ⲦⲀϨⲘ⸗, ⲦⲀϨⲘ̄†   *knock, invite, call;* m. *invitation,*
     calling

ⲐⲘⲞ   *warm* (caus. of ϨⲘⲞⲘ)

ⲐⲘ̄ⲔⲞ, ⲐⲘ̄ⲔⲈ-, ⲐⲘ̄ⲔⲞ⸗, ⲐⲘ̄ⲔⲎⲨ†   *afflict, humiliate*

ⲐⲘ̄ⲤⲞ, ⲐⲘ̄ⲤⲞ⸗, ⲐⲘ̄ⲤⲞⲈⲒⲦ†   *seat* (caus. of ϨⲘⲞⲞⲤ)

ⲐⲎⲚ   m. *sulphur* (ⲑⲉⲓ̈ⲟⲩ)

TE2NE f. *forehead*

ⲐⲚⲞ *crush* v. ⲦⲚ̄ⲚⲞ

ⲦⲌⲚⲞ, ⲐⲚⲞ, ⲦⲌⲚⲈ-, ⲦⲌⲚⲞ⸓, ⲐⲚⲎⲨ† *approach, hire*

ⲦⲌⲠⲞ, ⲐⲠⲞ⸓ [ⲦⲌⲠⲀ⸓] *cause to reach, escort, bring back* (caus. of ⲠⲰⲌ)

[ⲈⲢⲔⲞ] *calm* v. ⲌⲢ̄ⲞⲔ

ⲦⲌⲢⲰⲞ, ⲐⲢⲰⲞ *terrify*

ⲦⲰⲌⲤ, ⲦⲈⲌⲤ-, ⲦⲀⲌⲤ⸓, ⲦⲀⲌⲤ† *anoint;* m. *anointing, ointment*

ⲦⲀⲌⲦⲌ, ⲦⲈⲌⲦⲰⲌ⸓, ⲦⲈⲌⲦⲰⲌ† [ⲦⲈⲌⲦⲀⲌⲦ†] *mix, confuse*
   [†ⲦⲌ] f. *mixture*]

ⲐⲞⲞⲨⲦ name of 1st Egyptian month (Thoth), beginning August 29

ⲦⲀⲬⲞ [ⲦⲀⲬⲰ] *judge, condemn*

ⲦⲬⲀⲒⲞ, ⲬⲀⲒⲞ, ⲬⲀⲈⲒⲞ, [ⲬⲀⲈⲒⲀ⸓] *triumph* (caus. of ⲰⲀ *rise*)
   ⲦⲬⲀⲒⲞ ⲈⲂⲞⲖ *display*

ⲦⲀⲬⲢⲞ, ⲦⲀⲬⲢⲈ-, ⲦⲀⲬⲢⲞ⸓, ⲦⲀⲬⲢⲎⲨ† [ⲦⲀⲬⲢⲀⲈⲒⲦ†, ⲦⲀⲬⲢⲎⲞⲨⲦ†]
   establish, strengthen, be solid†; m. *firmness, strength*
   ⲌⲚ̄ⲞⲨⲦⲀⲬⲢⲞ *certainly*

ⲦⲰⲰⲂⲈ, ⲦⲰⲂⲈ, ⲦⲈⲂ-, ⲦⲈⲔ-, ⲦⲞⲞⲂ⸓, ⲦⲞⲂ⸓, ⲦⲞⲞⲔ⸓, ⲦⲎⲂ† *be joined, cling,*
   adhere, plant
   ⲦⲰⲰⲂⲈ ⲈⲂⲞⲖ *announce, publish*
   ⲢⲀⲦⲰⲂⲈ *joint* (ⲢⲀ)

ⲦⲂⲀⲒⲞ, ⲂⲀⲒⲞ, ⲦⲂⲀⲒⲈ-, ⲂⲀⲒⲈ-, ⲦⲂⲀⲒⲞ⸓, ⲂⲀⲒⲞ⸓, ⲦⲂⲀⲒ̈ⲎⲨ†, ⲂⲀⲒ̈ⲎⲨ† *condemn,*
   disgrace, be disgraced
   ⲂⲀⲒ̈Ⲉ m. *ugliness, disgrace*

ⲦⲰⲂ̄Ⲛ, ⲦⲀⲂⲚ⸓ *repel, thwart, push*

ⲦⲰⲂⲤ, ⲦⲞⲂⲤ⸓, ⲦⲞⲂⲤ† *bleach, dye*

ⲦⲀⲂⲤⲈ f. *sole of foot, footprint*

ⲦⲈⲂⲦⲰⲂ† *be pressed†*

ⲞⲨ, Ⲩ
called 2e transliterated *ou, u*

Ⲩ as number *four hundred*

ⲞⲨ is often treated as a consonant (Middle Egyptian *w*)

ⲞⲨ- indefinite article sing. *a, an* (ⲞⲨⲀ)
   The ⲟ elides when preceded by the I perfect conj. base Ⲁ- (ⲀⲨ-)
   The ⲟ elides when preceded by the preposition Ⲉ- [Ⲁ-] (ⲈⲨ- [ⲀⲨ-])

ⲞⲨ [Ⲱ, ⲈⲨ] *what?*
   ⲞⲨⲞⲨ with indefinite art.
   ⲈⲦⲂⲈⲞⲨ *why?*

-ⲞⲨ suffix pronoun 3rd person pl. *them*

ⲞⲨⲀ m. *blasphemy*
   ⲬⲈⲞⲨⲀ, ⲬⲒⲞⲨⲀ Ⲉ- *blaspheme against*

ⲞⲨⲀ [ⲞⲨⲈⲈⲒ], f. ⲞⲨⲈⲒ, ⲞⲨ-, -ⲞⲨⲈ m. *one, someone*
   ⲞⲨⲀ ⲞⲨⲀ *one by one*
   ⲠⲞⲨⲀ ⲠⲞⲨⲀ *each one*
   ⲔⲈⲞⲨⲀ *another one*

ⲞⲨⲀⲀ⸓, ⲞⲨⲀⲀⲦ⸓, ⲞⲨⲞⲞⲦ⸓, ⲞⲨⲀⲦ⸓ [ⲞⲨⲈⲦ⸓] *alone* v. ⲞⲨⲰⲦ

ⲞⲨⲈ [ⲞⲨⲀⲈⲒⲈ], ⲞⲨⲎⲨ† [ⲞⲨⲎⲞⲨ†] *be distant, far from, away;* m. *distance*

ⲘⲠⲞⲨⲈ   *at a distance, far away*
ⲞⲨⲞⲈⲓ [ⲞⲨⲀⲈⲓ] m. *rush*
    ϯⲞⲨⲞⲈⲓ   *seek*
    ϯⲠⲞⲨⲞⲈⲓ   *advance, approach, rush*
ⲞⲨⲞⲓ̈ [ⲞⲨⲀⲈⲓ] *woe!*
ⲞⲨⲞⲈⲓⲈ, pl. ⲞⲨⲈⲈⲓⲎ   m. *farmer*
[ⲞⲨⲞⲨ] v. ⲰⲰ   *conceive*
ⲞⲨⲰ   *finish*
    ⲞⲨⲰ   plus circumstantial *finish, already*
    ϯⲞⲨⲰ   *release, loose*
ⲞⲨⲰ   m. *news, report*
    ϤⲞⲨⲰ   *reply, answer, speak*
    ⲬⲠⲞⲨⲰ   *carry the news, announce*
ⲞⲨⲰ in ϯⲞⲨⲰ   *blossom, sprout*; m. *blossom, sprout*
    ⲬⲈⲞⲨⲰ, ⲬⲓⲞⲨⲰ   *conceive*
ⲞⲨⲀⲀⲂ† *be pure*† v. ⲞⲨⲞⲠ
ⲞⲨⲂⲈ-, ⲞⲨⲂⲎⲥ   *opposite, toward, against*
ⲞⲨⲂⲀϢ, ⲞⲨⲞⲂϢ† *become white, be white*†
    ⲞⲨⲰⲂϢ   *white*
ⲞⲨⲰⲰⲗⲈ, ⲞⲨⲰⲗⲈ, ⲞⲨⲞⲞⲗⲈ† *be well off, flourish*; m. *prosperity, plenty*
ⲞⲨⲰⲗⲤ, ⲞⲨⲈⲗⲤ-, ⲞⲨⲞⲗⲤⲥ, ⲞⲨⲞⲗⲤ† *bend, be bent*
    ⲞⲨⲰⲗⲤ ⲚϨⲎⲦ   *be discouraged*
ⲞⲨⲰⲘ, ⲞⲨⲞⲞⲘ, ⲞⲨⲘ̄-, ⲞⲨⲞⲘⲥ, p.c. ⲞⲨⲀⲘ-   *eat*
    ϬⲒⲚⲞⲨⲰⲘ, ⲬⲒⲚⲞⲨⲰⲘ, pl. ϬⲒⲚⲞⲨⲞⲞⲘ   m.f. *food, meal*
ⲞⲨⲰ(ⲱ)ⲘⲈ, ⲞⲨⲞⲞⲘⲥ   *accommodate, restrain oneself*
ⲞⲨⲘⲞⲦ, ⲞⲨⲞⲘⲦ† *thicken*
ⲞⲨⲞⲘϤ [ⲞⲨⲞⲚⲈϤ] m. *manger*
ⲞⲨⲚ̄-   existential predicate *there is, are* (neg. ⲘⲘⲚ̄-, q.v.)
    ⲞⲨⲚ̄- . . . ⲘⲘⲞⲥ   *have, has*
    ⲞⲨⲚ̄- . . . ϨⲒⲰⲰⲥ   *have, has*
    ⲞⲨⲚ̄ⲞⲨⲞⲚ Ⲉ-, ⲈⲢⲞⲥ   *have something against, be indebted to*
    ⲚⲈⲨⲚ̄-   *there was* (ⲚⲈ ⲞⲨⲚ̄-)
    ⲞⲨⲚ̄ⲦⲈ-, ⲞⲨⲚ̄Ⲧⲥ, ⲞⲨⲚ̄ⲦⲀⲥ   *have, has* (ⲞⲨⲚ̄- Ⲛ̄ⲦⲈ-)
    neg. (Ⲙ̄)ⲘⲚ̄ⲦⲈ-, (Ⲙ̄)ⲘⲚ̄ⲦⲀⲥ   *have not, has not*
    ⲞⲨⲚ̄ⲦⲈ- . . . Ⲉ-, ⲈⲢⲞⲥ   *be indebted to*
ⲞⲨⲞⲈⲓⲚ [ⲞⲨⲞⲈⲒⲚⲈ, ⲞⲨⲀⲈⲒⲚ] m. *light*
    ϤⲞⲨⲞⲈⲒⲚ   *shine*
ⲞⲨⲞⲚ [ⲞⲨⲀⲚ] *someone, something*
    ⲞⲨⲞⲚ ⲚⲒⲘ   *everyone*
ⲞⲨⲰⲚ, ⲞⲨⲎⲚ [ⲞⲨⲈⲚ], ⲞⲨⲎⲚ† *open, be open*
    imper. ⲀⲞⲨⲰⲚ, ⲀⲨⲰⲚ [ⲀⲨⲞⲨⲰⲚ], ⲞⲨⲚ-
ⲞⲨⲰⲚ, ⲞⲨⲚ̄-   m. *part*
    followed by a number: ⲞⲨⲰⲚ Ⲛ̄ϢⲞⲘⲚ̄Ⲧ *a third part*
ⲞⲨⲈⲒⲚⲈ   *pass by*
ⲞⲨⲚⲀⲘ [ⲞⲨⲚⲈⲘ] f. *right hand, right*
ⲞⲨⲈⲈⲓⲈⲚⲒⲚ [ⲞⲨⲀⲈⲒⲀⲚⲒⲚ] n. *Ionian, Greek*
    Ⲙ̄Ⲛ̄ⲦⲞⲨⲈⲈⲒⲈⲚⲒⲚ   f. *Greek language*
ⲞⲨⲚⲞⲨ, pl. ⲞⲨⲚⲞⲞⲨⲈ   f. *hour*
    Ⲛ̄ⲦⲈⲨⲚⲞⲨ   *immediately* (o eliding)

τενογ, †νογ *now*

τενογ, †νογ *nowογωνϣ* m. *wolf*

ογνοϥ [ογναϥ] *rejoice;* m. *joy*

ογωνς, ογενς-, ογονς⸗ [ογανς⸗], ογονςⲧ [ογανςⲧ] (εβολ) *show, reveal, be revealed, be manifest, appear;* m. *appearance, revelation*

ογοπ, ογααβⲧ [ογααϥⲧ] *be pure, innocent, pureⲧ, holyⲧ;* m. *purity*

　πετογααβ m. *saint*

　ογηηβ m. *priest*

ογηρ *how great?, how many?, how much?*

　αογηρ *about how much?*

ογⲣⲧ m. *rose*

ογⲣⲟⲧ [ογⲣⲁⲧ], ⲣⲟογⲧⲧ [ⲣⲁογⲧⲧ] *be glad, eager, ready, gladⲧ, freshⲧ, flourishingⲧ;* m. *zeal*

ογεⲣⲏⲧε, ογⲣⲏⲧε [ογⲣⲓⲧε] f. *foot, leg*

ογⲣϭϣε f. *watch, watchtower*

　ⲁⲛογⲣϭϣε m. *watchman*

ογⲱⲣⲥ, ογⲟⲣ⸗, ογⲟⲣⲥⲧ *set free, open*

ογⲉⲓⲥⲉ, ογⲁⲥⲧ⸗ *saw, chisel off*

ογⲟⲥⲧⲛ̄, ογⲉⲥⲧⲱⲛⲧ *broaden*

ογⲱⲥϥ, ογⲉⲥϥ- ογⲟⲥϥ⸗, ογⲟⲥϥⲧ [ογⲁⲥϥⲧ] *be idle, leave barren, annul, neglect;* m. *idleness, laziness*

ογⲱⲧ, ογⲉⲧ-, ογⲉⲧ⸗ *be raw, fresh, green*

　ογⲟ(ⲟ)ⲧⲉ m. *greens, herbs*

　ογⲟⲧⲟγⲉⲧ, ογⲉⲧⲟγⲱⲧⲧ *be green*

ογⲱⲧ, f. ογⲱⲧⲉ *single, alone, one, same*

　ογⲁⲁ⸗, ογⲁⲁⲧ⸗, ογⲟⲟⲧ⸗ [ογⲁⲉⲧ⸗], (ογⲁⲧ- [ογⲉⲧ-] with ⲑⲏγⲧⲛ̄) *alone, only, self*

　ⲙⲁγⲁⲁ⸗, ⲙⲁγⲁⲁⲧ⸗ (ⲙⲁγⲁⲧ- with ⲑⲏγⲧⲛ̄) *alone, only, self*

ογⲧⲉ-, ογⲇⲉ-, ογⲧⲱ⸗ *between, among*

ογⲱⲧⲉ, ογⲟⲧ⸗, ογⲟⲟⲧⲉⲧ [ογⲁⲁⲧⲧ] *send, separate, be differentⲧ, in exileⲧ*

　ογⲱⲧ, ογⲉⲧ *it is different*

　ογⲉⲧ . . . ογⲉⲧ . . . *one is . . . another is . . .*

ογⲱⲧⲃ̄, ογⲉⲧⲃ-, ογⲟⲧⲃ⸗, ογⲟⲧⲃ̄ⲧ [ογⲁⲧⲃ̄ⲧ, ογⲁⲧⲃⲉⲧ] *change, pass, cross, transfer, pierce, surpassⲧ, be superiorⲧ*

　ογⲁⲧⲃⲉ, ογⲁⲧϥⲉ f. *hole*

ογⲱⲧⲛ̄, ογⲟⲧⲛ⸗ *pour*

ογⲧⲁⲥ m. *fruit*

ογⲱⲧⲥ, ⲱⲧⲥ, ⲟⲧⲥ⸗ *pour, melt*

ογⲟⲉⲓϣ [ογⲁⲉⲓϣ] m. *occasion, time*

ογⲱϣ, ογⲱϣⲉ, ογⲉϣ-, ογⲁϣ⸗, ογⲟϣ⸗ *desire, wish, want;* m. *desire, love, will*

ογⲱϣ m. *gap, pause*

　ⲛ̄ογⲉϣ [ογϣ] ⲛ̄- *without*

ογϣⲏ f. *night*

　ⲛ̄ⲧⲉγϣⲏ *by night*

ογⲱϣⲉ *consume*

ογⲱϣⲃ̄, ογⲉϣⲃ-, ογⲟϣⲃ⸗ *answer, reply, respond*

ογⲱϣⲙ̄, ογⲟϣⲙ⸗, ογⲟϣⲙ̄ⲧ *knead;* m. *dough*

ογϣⲁⲡ [ογϣⲉⲡ] m. *loan*

† ⲉⲡⲟⲩⲱⲁⲡ *lend*

ⲟⲩⲱⲱⲥ, ⲟⲩⲉⲱⲥ-, ⲟⲩⲟⲱⲥ⸗, ⲟⲩⲟⲱⲥᵗ   *be broad, widen, be at ease;*
   m. *breadth*

   ⲟⲩⲱⲱⲥ ⲉⲃⲟⲗ   *spread out, open wide*

ⲟⲩⲱⲱⲧ   *worship, greet*

ⲟⲩⲱⲱϥ, ⲟⲩⲉⲱϥ, ⲟⲩⲟⲱϥ⸗, ⲟⲩⲟⲱϥᵗ   *be worn down, crushed, perish, break;*
   m. *breakage, destruction*

ⲟⲩⲱϩ [ⲟⲩϩⲱϩ], ⲟⲩⲉϩ-, ⲟⲩⲁϩ⸗ [ⲟⲩϩⲁ⸗], ⲟⲩⲏϩᵗ, p.c. ⲟⲩⲁϩ-   *put, place,*
   *set, lay, dwell, rest*ᵗ, *inhabit*ᵗ

   ⲟⲩⲱϩ ⲉⲧⲟⲟⲧ⸗   *add, repeat, continue*

   ⲟⲩⲱϩ ⲉⲝⲛ̄-   *add to*

   ⲟⲩⲱϩ ⲛ̄-   *add to*

   ⲟⲩⲁϩ⸗ (reflexive) ⲛ̄ⲥⲁ-   *follow*

   ⲟⲩⲱϩ ⲛ̄ⲧⲛ̄-   *pledge to*

   ⲟⲩⲱϩ ⲉⲃⲟⲗ   *set down, pause, let down*

   ⲟⲩⲉϩⲥⲁϩⲛⲉ   *command* v. ⲥⲁϩⲛⲉ

[ⲟⲩϩⲉ] v. ϩⲟⲩϩⲉ   *miscarriage*

[ⲟⲩⲓϩⲉ], ⲟⲩⲟϩⲉᵗ, p.c. ⲟⲩⲁϩⲓ-   *miss, be unsuccessful*

   ⲟⲩⲁϩⲓϩⲏⲧ, ⲟⲩⲁϩⲓⲏⲧ   *cruel*

ⲟⲩⲟⲟϩⲉ   f. *scorpion*

ⲟⲩⲱϩⲉ   m. *fisherman*

ⲟⲩⲱϩⲙ̄, ⲟⲩⲉϩⲙ-, ⲟⲩⲁϩⲙ⸗, ⲟⲩⲟϩⲙ̄ᵗ   *repeat, answer, reply, translate;*
   m. *answer, interpretation*

ⲟⲩϩⲟⲣ, pl. ⲟⲩϩⲟⲟⲣ   m.f. *dog*

ⲟⲩⲭⲁⲓ̈ [ⲟⲩⲭⲉⲉⲓ, ⲟⲩⲭⲁⲉⲓⲧⲉ], ⲟⲩⲟⲭᵗ [ⲟⲩⲁⲭᵗ]   *be whole, be safe, be*
   *healthy*ᵗ, *saved*ᵗ; m. *salvation*

ⲟⲩⲟ̄ⲃⲉ   f. *jaw, cheek*

ⲟⲩⲱϭⲡ, ⲟⲩⲉϭⲡ-, ⲟⲩⲟϭⲡ⸗   *break, be broken*

ⲟⲩⲱϭⲥ   *collect;* m. *collection*

ⲟⲩⲟϭⲟⲩⲉϭ, ⲟⲩⲉϭⲟⲩⲱϭ⸗   *chew, crush*

ϕ
called ϕⲓ   transliterated *ph*

ϕ̄   as number *five hundred*
ϕ   for ⲡϩ, sometimes the def. art. sing. masc. before words with initial ϩ or
   Gk. words with rough breathing

x
called ⲭⲓ   transliterated *ch*

x̄   as number *six hundred*
x   rare except in words of Gk. derivation

ψ

called ψι   transliterated *ps*

Ψ̄   as number *seven hundred*
ψ   for πс, otherwise only in words of Gk. derivation

ⲱ

called ⲱ   transliterated *ō*

Ⲱ̄   as number *eight hundred*
ⲱ   *O!*
ⲱⲱ, ⲱ [ⲟⲩⲟⲩ], ⲉⲉⲧ† *conceive, be pregnant*†
ⲱⲃⲱ, ⲉⲃⲱ-, ⲟⲃⲱ⸗ [ⲁⲃⲱ⸗], ⲟⲃⲱ† [ⲁⲃⲉⲱ†] *forget, neglect, be forgotten, sleep;* m. *sleep*
    ⲣ̄ⲡⲱⲃⲱ   *forget, be forgotten*
    ⲃ̄ⲱⲉ   f. *forgetfulness, oblivion, sleep*
ⲱⲕ (ⲛ̄ϩⲏⲧ) *be content;* [m. *pleasure*]
ⲱⲕⲙ̄, ⲉⲕⲙ-, ⲟⲕⲙ̄† [ⲁⲕⲙ̄†] *be gloomy, sad*
ⲱⲗ, ⲟⲗ-, ⲟⲗ⸗, ⲏⲗ† *hold, contain, gather*
    ⲱⲗ ⲉϩⲟⲩⲛ   *bring in, harvest*
    ⲱⲗ ⲉϩⲣⲁⲓ̈   *withdraw, ascend*
ⲱⲗⲕ, ⲗ̄ⲕ-, ⲟⲗⲕ⸗, ⲟⲗⲕ† *be bent, bent*†*, distorted*†*, bend oneself*
    ⲗ̄ⲕⲱⲁ   *turn up nose, sneer*
ⲱⲗⲙ̄, ⲟⲗⲙ⸗, ⲟⲗⲙ̄† *embrace*
ⲱⲙⲕ [ⲱⲙⲛ̄ⲕ], ⲉⲙⲕ-, ⲟⲙⲕ⸗ *swallow*
ⲱⲙⲥ, ⲉⲙⲥ-, ⲟⲙⲥ⸗, ⲟⲙⲥ† *be sunk, sink, dip;* m. *baptism*
ⲱⲛⲉ [ⲱⲱⲛⲉ], ⲉⲛⲉ- m.f. *stone*
    ⲉⲛⲉⲙ̄ⲙⲉ   *precious jewel* (ⲙⲉ *truth*)
ⲱⲛⲱ, ⲟⲛⲱ† *be astonished, amazed, dumbfounded*
ⲱⲛϩ, ⲱⲛⲁϩ [ⲱⲱⲛϩ], ⲟⲛϩ†, ⲟⲛⲁϩ† [ⲁⲛϩ†, ⲁⲁⲛϩ†] *live, be alive*†*;* m. *life*
ⲱⲡ, ⲉⲡ-, ⲟⲡ⸗ [ⲁⲡ⸗], ⲏⲡ† *count, calculate, consider, be counted*†*, reckoned*†*, belong*†
    ⲏⲡⲉ   f. *number*
ⲱⲣⲃ̄, ⲱⲣϥ, ⲉⲣⲃ-, ⲟⲣⲃ⸗, ⲟⲣⲃ̄† *restrict, surround, enclose*
    ⲣ̄ⲃⲉ   f. *enclosure, pen*
ⲱⲣⲕ, ⲟⲣⲕ⸗ *swear, invoke;* m. *oath*
ⲱⲣⲱ, ⲟⲣⲱ† *be cold*
ⲱⲣⲝ, ⲟⲩⲱⲣⲝ, ⲣ̄ⲝ-, ⲟⲣⲝ† [ⲁⲣⲉⲝ†] *be firm, secure, confirm, fasten, imprison;* m. *firmness, assurance*
ⲱⲥⲕ, ⲟⲥⲕ† *delay, continue, spend time*
[ⲱⲥϩ] v. ⲱϩⲥ *reap*
ⲱⲥϭ, ⲱϭⲥ, ⲟⲥϭ† *anoint*
ⲱⲧⲡ, ⲉⲧⲡ-, ⲟⲧⲡ⸗ [ⲁⲧⲡ⸗], ⲟⲧⲡ† *shut, enclose, imprison*
ⲱⲧⲡ, ⲁⲧⲡ-, ⲟⲧⲡ⸗, ⲟⲧⲡ† *load*
    ⲉⲧⲡⲱ   f. *burden*
ⲱⲧϩ, ⲟⲧϩ† *tie, sew, weave*
ⲱⲧϩ v. ⲟⲩⲱⲧϩ *pour*
ⲱⲱ, ⲉⲱ-, ⲁⲱ-, ⲟⲱ⸗ [ⲁⲱ⸗] *call, announce, read, promise;* m. *reading*

ⲱϣ ⲉⲃⲟⲗ *call out*
(ⲱϣ) ⲟϣ⳿,ⲣⲟϣ⳿,ⲟⲛϣ⳿ (ⲉⲣⲟⲩⲛ) *slide oneself in, slither oneself into*
ⲱϣⲙ̄,ⲉϣⲙ-,ⲟϣⲙ⳿,ⲟϣⲙ̄† *extinguish, quench, be quenched*
ⲱϭⲉ,ⲱⲃⲉ,ⲟϥ⳿ [ⲁⲃ⳿] *press*
ⲱϭⲧ,ⲉϥⲧ-,ⲟϥⲧ⳿ [ⲁϥⲧ⳿],ⲟϥⲧ† *nail, attach*
  ⲉⲓϥⲧ,ⲉⲓⲃⲧ m. *nail*
  ϣⲥⲛ̄ⲉⲓϥⲧ [ϣⲱϥⲧ] m. *nail wound* (ⲥⲱϣ)
ⲱⲣⲉ,ⲟⲣⲉ,ⲁⲣⲉ† *stand, stay, wait*
  ⲁⲣⲉⲣⲁⲧ⳿ *stand oneself* (ⲁⲣⲉ ⲉⲣⲁⲧ⳿ v.ⲣⲁⲧ⳿)
  ⲁⲣⲉ ⲛ̄- *need*
ⲱⲣⲥ [ⲱⲥⲣ],ⲉⲣⲥ-,ⲟⲣⲥ⳿ [ⲁⲣⲥ⳿,ⲣⲁⲥ⳿] *reap, mow;* m. *harvest*
  ⲟⲣⲥ [ⲁⲥⲣ] m. *sickle*
  ⲭⲁⲓ̈ⲟⲣⲥ m. *harvester*
ⲱⲝ n. *thief*
ⲱⲝⲛ̄ [ⲱⲝⲛⲉ],ⲉⲝⲛ- [ⲁⲝⲛ-],ⲟⲝⲛ⳿ *stop, do away with, annihilate, destroy;* m. *destruction*
ⲱϭ̄ⲃ,ⲣⲱϭ̄ⲃ,ⲣⲟⲟϭ̄ⲃ†,ⲟⲃϥ† *be cold, frozen;* [ⲣⲟⲟⲃⲉⲥ] m. *cold, frost*
ⲱϭⲥ v.ⲱⲥϭ *anoint*
ⲱϭⲧ,ⲟϭⲧ⳿ *choke, strangle*

ϣ
called ϣⲁⲓ transliterated š

[ϣ for Gk. rough breathing (rare)]
ϣ-,ⲉϣ- vb. aux. *be able to, can*
[ϣⲁ-] v.ⲉ⳿ ϣⲁⲛ- conj. base conditional
ϣⲁ-,ϣⲁⲣⲟ⳿ [ϣⲁⲣⲁ⳿] *to, toward, as far as, until*
ϣⲁ [ϣⲁⲉⲓⲉ] *rise* (sun), *shine*
  ⲙ̄ⲙⲁⲛ̄ϣⲁ *the east* (pl. art.)
  ϣⲁ m. *festival*
  ⲣ̄ϣⲁ *celebrate a festival*
ϣⲁ,ϣⲉ [ϣⲁⲉⲓ],ϣⲁⲛⲧ⳿ m. *nose*
ϣⲁ⳿,ϣⲁⲣⲉ- conjugation base habitual present
  ⲉϣⲁ⳿,ⲉϣⲁⲣⲉ- relative of habitual present *who, which usually,* or circumstantial
ϣⲁⲓ̈ *new*
ϣⲉ, [imper.ⲙⲁϣⲉ] *go*
  ϣⲉⲉⲓ *move to and fro, wander* (ⲉⲓ *come*)
ϣⲉ m. *wood, cross*
  ϩⲁⲙϣⲉ m. *carpenter*
ϣⲉ *hundred*
ϣⲉ,ϣⲁ *by* in swearing
ϣⲉ *pig* v.ⲉϣⲱ
ϣⲉ v.ϣϣⲉ *be suitable*
ϣⲏⲓ̈ m. *cistern, well*
ϣⲓ,ϣⲓⲧ⳿,ϣⲏⲩ† *measure, weigh;* m. *measure, weight, amount*
ϣⲓⲁⲓ̈,ϣⲟⲓ̈† *be long;* m. *length*
  ϣⲓ̈ⲏ f. *length*

ϣⲱⲓ̈ m. *height, above*

ϣⲟ *thousand*

ϣⲟ *indeed*

ϣⲱ [ϣⲟⲩ] m. *sand*

ϣⲱⲃ, ϣⲱϥ, ϣⲃ̄-, ϣⲏⲃⁱ *shave*

ϣⲃⲉ v. ϣϥⲉ *seventy*

ϣⲏⲃⲉ m. *rust*

ϣⲃⲉ, ϣϥⲉ n. *scum, filth*

ϣⲓⲃⲉ [ϣⲓⲃⲏ, ϣϥⲉⲓⲉ], ϣⲃ̄-, ϣⲃⲧ⸗, ϣϥⲧ⸗, ϣⲟⲃⲉⁱ, p.c. ϣⲁⲃⲉ- *change, transform, be changed, different*ⁱ; m. *change, difference*

ϣⲃ̄ⲓⲟ, ϣⲉⲃⲓⲏⲩⁱ, ϣⲃ̄ⲃⲓⲁⲉⲓⲧⁱ [ϣⲃ̄ⲃⲓⲏⲟⲩⲧⁱ, ϣⲃ̄ⲃⲓⲟⲉⲓⲧⁱ] *change, be changed*ⁱ, *different*ⁱ

ϣⲃⲉⲓⲱ, ϣⲃ̄ⲃⲓⲱ, ϣⲉⲃⲓⲱ [ϫⲃ̄ⲃⲓⲱ] f. *substitution, exchange*

ϣⲃⲱ [ϣⲃⲱⲱⲥ] v. ϣϥⲱ *myth*

ϣⲃⲏⲣ, ϣⲃⲣ̄, f. ϣⲃⲉⲉⲣⲉ, pl. ϣⲃⲉⲉⲣ *friend, comrade, partner*

ϣⲃⲣ̄- *companion in, fellow, co-*

ⲣ̄- (ⲟⁱ ⲛ̄-) ϣⲃⲏⲣ *be a friend, partner, join in*

ϣⲃⲱⲧ m. *rod, staff*

ϣⲱⲃϩ v. ϣⲱϩⲃ̄ *be withered*

ϣⲱⲕ, ϣⲉⲕ-, ϣⲏⲕⁱ *dig, be deep, deep*ⁱ

ϣⲓⲕⲉ, ϣⲉⲕⲧ-, ϣⲁⲕⲧ⸗, ϣⲟⲕⲉⁱ *dig;* m. *depth*

ϣⲓⲕ m. *depth*

ϣⲕⲁⲕ m. *call, shout*

ⲁϣⲕⲁⲕ ⲉⲃⲟⲗ *call out* (ⲱϣ)

ϫⲓϣⲕⲁⲕ ⲉⲃⲟⲗ *call out* (ϫⲱ)

ϣⲕⲟⲗ m. *hole*

ϣⲱⲕϩ, ϣⲟⲕϩⁱ *dig, be deep* (ϣⲱⲕ)

ϣⲁⲗ m. *myrrh*

ϣⲟⲗ m. *tooth, tusk*

ϣⲟⲗ m. *bundle*

ϣⲱⲗ, ϣⲉⲗ-, ϣⲟⲗ⸗, p.c. ϣⲁⲗ- *plunder, destroy;* m. *booty*

ϣⲱⲗ, ϣⲟⲗ⸗, ϣⲏⲗⁱ *flow, loosen, dissolve*

ϣⲱⲗⲕ *weave*

ϣⲗⲏⲗ, ϣⲗⲁ̄ *pray;* m. *prayer*

ϣⲱⲗⲙ̄ *smell*

[ϣⲱⲗⲙ̄ *draw out* (sword)]

[ϣⲗ̄ⲙⲉ f. *kindling, particle*]

ϣⲟⲗⲙⲉⲥ f. *gnat*

ϣⲗⲟⲡ m. *strand*

ϣⲉⲗⲉⲉⲧ f. *bride, marriage*

ⲙⲁⲛ̄ϣⲉⲗⲉⲉⲧ m. *bridal chamber*

ⲡⲁⲧϣⲉⲗⲉⲉⲧ m. *bridegroom* (ⲡⲁ poss.)

ϫⲓϣⲉⲗⲉⲉⲧ *marry*

ϣⲗⲟϥ m. *shame, disgrace, shameful*

[ϣⲁⲗⲉϥⁱ *shameful*ⁱ]

ϣⲗ̄ϩ m. *twig, shoot*

ϣⲱⲗϩ, ϣⲟⲗϩ⸗, ϣⲟⲗϩⁱ *make a mark, trace a line;* m. *mark, stake*

ϣⲗⲁϩ, ϣⲟⲗϩⁱ *be afraid*

ϣⲗⲁϥ ⲓⲛ ⲛⲉϩϣⲗⲁϥ *shudder, be terrified* (ⲛⲟⲩϩⲉ)

ϢⲦⲂ̄ⲞⲘ, ⲤⲈⲖⲂⲀⲘ, ϢⲦⲀⲘ, ϢⲀⲀⲦⲘ̄, ϢⲦⲎⲘ, ϢⲦⲎ̄ m.f. *mustard, turnip*

ϢⲎⲘ, ϢⲎ̄ *small, little, young, few*

   ϢⲎⲘ ϢⲎⲘ *little by little*

ϢⲞⲘ, ϢⲰⲞⲘ, f. ϢⲰⲘⲈ m. *father-(son-)in-law*, f. *mother- (daughter-) in-law*

ϢⲰⲘ, [f. ϢⲀⲘⲎ] m. *summer*

   ϢⲰⲘ m. *tribute, tax, rent* (i.e. harvest tax)

ϢⲰⲰⲘⲈ, ϢⲰⲘⲈ f. *cliff*

ϢⲘⲀ, ϢⲞⲞⲘⲉ† *be light, fine, subtle*

ϢⲘⲞⲨ, ϢⲘⲞⲨⲈ f. *peg, stake*

ϢⲘ̄ⲘⲞ, f. ϢⲘ̄ⲘⲰ, pl. ϢⲘ̄ⲘⲞⲒ [ϢⲘ̄ⲘⲀⲈⲒ] n. *stranger, visitor, alien*

   ⲘⲀⲒϢⲘ̄ⲘⲞ *hospitable*

   Ⲣ̄- (ⲟ† Ⲛ̄-) ϢⲘ̄ⲘⲞ *become a stranger, alienated*

ϢⲘⲞⲨⲚ, f. ϢⲘⲞⲨⲚⲈ, -ϢⲘⲎⲚⲈ *eight*

   Ⲍ̄ⲘⲈⲚⲈ *eighty*

ϢⲞⲘⲚ̄Ⲧ [ϢⲀⲘⲚ̄Ⲧ], ϢⲞⲘⲦ, f. ϢⲞⲘⲦⲈ, ϢⲘ̄Ⲧ-, ϢⲘⲚ̄Ⲧ- [ϢⲚ̄Ⲧ-], -ϢⲞⲘⲦⲈ *three*

   ⲘⲈⲌϢⲞⲘⲚ̄Ⲧ *third*

ϢⲘ̄ϢⲈ, ϢⲘ̄ϢⲈ-, ϢⲘ̄ϢⲎⲦ⸍ *serve, worship;* m. *service, worship*

ϢⲀⲚ- forms conj. base conditional v. ⲉ⸍ ϢⲀⲚ-

ϢⲎⲚ m. *tree*

   ϢⲚⲎ f. *garden, orchard*

ϢⲒⲚⲈ, ϢⲈⲚ-, ϢⲚ̄Ⲧ⸍ *seek, ask*

   ϢⲒⲚⲈ, ϢⲚ̄- m. *inquiry, news*

   ϢⲒⲚⲈ ⲉ- *greet, visit*

   ϢⲒⲚⲈ Ⲛ̄ⲤⲀ-, Ⲛ̄ⲤⲰ⸍ *seek*

   ϢⲘ̄ⲚⲞⲨϥⲈ m. *good news*

   ⲢⲈϥϢⲒⲚⲈ n. *diviner, fortune-teller*

   ϬⲒⲚⲈ Ⲙ̄ⲠϢⲒⲚⲈ, ϬⲘ̄ⲠϢⲒⲚⲈ *visit*

   ϥⲀⲒϢⲒⲚⲈ m. *messenger*

ϢⲰⲚⲈ [ϢⲞⲚⲈ], ϢⲞⲞⲚⲉ† *be sick, weak;* ϢⲚ̄-, ϢⲈⲚ-, ϢⲀⲚ- m. *sickness, disease, weakness*

ϢⲰⲰⲚⲈ, ϢⲈⲈⲚⲈ-, ϢⲞ(Ⲟ)Ⲛ⸍, ϢⲞⲞⲚⲉ† *exclude, be deprived*†

ϢⲚⲀ m. *prodigal, waste*

   ⲘⲚ̄ⲦϢⲚⲀ f. *profligacy, intemperance*

ϢⲚⲈ, pl. ϢⲚⲎⲨ m. *net*

ϢⲚ̄Ⲥ m. *linen*

ϢⲰⲚⲦ, ϢⲚ̄Ⲧ-, ϢⲞⲚⲦ⸍, ϢⲞⲚⲦ† *plait, weave* (mats, wreaths, baskets)

   ϢⲞⲚⲦⲈ f. *plaited work*

ϢⲀⲚⲦ⸍, ϢⲀⲚⲦⲈ- conjugation base *until*

ϢⲞⲚⲦⲈ [ϢⲀⲚⲦⲈ] f. *thorn bush, acacia*

ϢⲚ̄ⲦⲰ f. *linen robe, sheet*

ϢⲰⲚϥ, ϢⲰⲚⲂ̄, ϢⲈⲚϥ-, ϢⲞⲚϥ⸍, ϢⲞⲚⲂ⸍, ϢⲞⲚϥ† *join, come together;* m. *union*

ϢⲞⲠ, ϢⲰⲠ m. *palm, four-fingerbreadth, four*

ϢⲰⲠ, ϢⲠ-, ϢⲈⲠ-, ϢⲞⲠ⸍ [ϢⲀⲠ⸍], ϢⲎⲠ† *receive, take, get, buy, be accepted*†, *acceptable*†

   ϢⲞⲠⲤ f. *reception, banquet*

   ϢⲠϢⲠ-, ϢⲠϢⲰⲠ⸍ *embrace*

ϢⲰⲠ in Ⲍ̄ⲚⲞⲨϢⲠ̄Ⲛ̄ϢⲰⲠ *suddenly*

ϣⲓⲡⲉ *be ashamed, shame;* m. *shame*
  ϣⲓⲡⲉ ϩⲏⲧ⸗ ⲛ- *be ashamed before*
  ϯϣⲓⲡⲉ *put to shame*
  ϫⲓϣⲓⲡⲉ *be ashamed*
ϣⲱⲡⲉ, ϣⲟⲟⲡᵗ *become, come about, happen, be*ᵗ, *exist*ᵗ, *dwell*ᵗ; [m. *being*]
  ϣⲱⲡⲉ ⲉ- *become*
  ϣⲱⲡⲉ (ϣⲟⲟⲡᵗ) ⲛ- *become (be*ᵗ)
  ϣⲱⲡⲉ (ϣⲟⲟⲡᵗ) ⲛⲁ⸗ *get, have*ᵗ
  ⲙⲁ ⲛϣⲱⲡⲉ m. *dwelling place, cell* of a monk
  ⲉϣⲱⲡⲉ [ⲉϣⲡⲉ, ⲉⲓϣⲡⲉ, ϣⲡⲉ] *if, when, since, because*
  ⲉϣⲱⲡⲉ ⲙ̄ⲙⲟⲛ *if not, otherwise*
  [ⲡⲉⲧϣⲟⲟⲡ m. *the One who exists*]
  [ϣ̄ⲣⲡ̄ⲛϣⲱⲡⲉ *pre-exist*]
[ϣⲡⲱⲡ *promise;* m. *promise* (ϣⲱⲡ plus ⲱⲡ)]
ϣⲡⲏⲣⲉ f. *wonder, amazement, omen*
  ⲣ̄ϣⲡⲏⲣⲉ *be amazed, marvel*
ϣⲱⲡϣ m. *arm, shoulder*
ϣⲁⲁⲣ [ϣⲁⲁⲣⲉ, ϣⲉⲗ] m. *skin, hide*
  ⲃⲁⲕϣⲁⲁⲣ m. *tanner*
ϣⲁⲁⲣ m. *price*
ϣⲁⲣⲉ- v. ϣⲁ⸗ conj. base habitual present
ϣⲁⲁⲣⲉ, ϣⲁⲁⲣ, ϣⲁⲡᵗ *hit, strike*
  ⲣⲉϥϣⲁⲁⲣ m. *demon*
ϣⲏⲣⲉ, ϣⲣ̄- [ϣⲏⲣ-], ϣⲉ-, ϣⲛ̄-, f. ϣⲉⲉⲣⲉ [ϫⲉⲣⲉ] m. *son, child,* f. *daughter*
  ϣⲏⲣⲉ ϣⲏⲙ m. *child, baby, youth*
  ϣⲛ̄ⲟⲩⲁ, ϣⲟⲩⲟⲩⲁ, ϣⲟⲩⲁ m.f. *cousin*
ϣⲓⲣⲉ *small, little*
  ϩⲣ̄ϣⲓⲣⲉ m. *youth, young servant* (ϩⲁⲗ)
ϣⲱⲣⲡ, ϣⲣ̄ⲡ-, ϣⲟⲣⲡ⸗ *be early*
  ϣⲣ̄ⲡ- plus verb *first, before, already*
  ϣⲱⲣⲡ m. *morning*
  ϣⲟⲣⲡ [ϣⲁⲣⲡ], ϣⲣ̄ⲡ-, f. ϣⲟⲣⲡⲉ m. *earliest, first*
  ⲛ̄ϣⲱⲣⲡ, ⲛ̄ϣⲟⲣⲡ *early, first of all, before*
  ϫⲓⲛⲛ̄ϣⲟⲣⲡ *from the beginning*
  ⲣ̄ϣⲟⲣⲡ *precede, hurry*
  ⲣ̄ϣⲟⲣⲡ ⲛ- plus verb *first, pre-, pro-, fore-, already*
ϣⲟⲣϣ̄ [ϣⲁⲣϣ̄], ϣⲣ̄ϣⲱⲣ⸗, ϣⲣ̄ϣⲱⲣᵗ *upset, overturn;* m. *destruction*
ϣⲉⲥ-, ϣⲥ- v. ⲥⲱϣ *strike*
ϣⲱⲥ, ϣⲏⲥᵗ v. ⲥⲱϣ *despise*
ϣⲱⲥ, pl. ϣⲟⲟⲥ m. *flock, herd, shepherd*
ϣⲱⲥⲙ̄ v. ⲥⲱϣⲙ̄ *be faint*
ϣⲥⲛⲉ [ⲥϣⲛⲉ, ϣⲛⲉ] m. *moment*
  ϩⲛ̄ⲟⲩϣⲥⲛⲉ [ⲁⲡⲥϣⲛⲉ] *suddenly*
ϣⲏⲧ *two hundred*
ϣⲓⲏⲧ *Scete,* a desolate place near the Wadi Natrun south of Alexandria
ϣⲟⲧ, ϣⲱⲧ, pl. ϣϣⲱⲧⲉ m. *pillow, cushion*
ϣⲱⲧ, ⲉϣⲱⲧ, ⲉϣⲱⲱⲧ, pl. ⲉϣⲟⲧⲉ m. *trader, merchant*
ϣⲱⲱⲧ, ϣⲱⲧ, ϣ(ⲉ)ⲧ-, ϣⲉⲉⲧ-, ϣⲁⲁⲧ⸗, ϣⲁⲧ⸗, ϣⲁⲁⲧᵗ, ϣⲁⲧᵗ,
  p.c. ϣⲁⲧ- *cut, sacrifice, lack, fall short*ᵗ, *be lacking*ᵗ; m. *sacrifice, need,*

deficiency

ϣⲱⲱⲧ ⲉⲃⲟⲗ cut off, decide; m. *excommunication*

ϣⲁⲧⲛ̅- except, minus

ϣⲁⲁⲧⲉ f. *portion*

ϣⲁⲁⲧⲥ f. *cutting, ditch*

ϩⲓϣⲁⲁⲧⲥ ⲉ- break in

ϣⲧⲁ m. *deficiency, fault*

ϣⲓⲧⲉ, ϣⲱⲧ, ϣⲁⲧⲉ demand, extort

ϣⲱⲧⲉ f. *well, cistern, pit*

ϣⲱⲧⲉ m. *flour, dough*

ϣⲧⲉ m. *mast, pole*

ϣⲧⲟ, ϣⲧⲏⲩ⁺ v. ⲭⲧⲟ lay down

ϣⲱⲧⲃ̅, ϣⲉⲧⲃ- muzzle

ϣⲧⲉⲕⲟ, pl. ϣⲧⲉⲕⲱⲟⲩ m. *prison*

ϣⲱⲧⲙ̅, ϣⲧⲙ-, ϣⲟⲧⲙ̅⁺ shut, be shut

  ϣⲧⲁⲙ [ϣⲧⲉⲙ], ϣⲧⲁⲙ- shut, close

ϣⲧⲏⲛ f. *garment, tunic*

ϣⲧⲟⲣⲧⲣ̅ [ϣⲧⲁⲣⲧⲣ̅], ϣⲧⲣ̅ⲧⲣ-, ϣⲧⲣ̅ⲧⲱⲣⲉ, ϣⲧⲣ̅ⲧⲱⲣⲧ⁺
  [ϣⲧⲣ̅ⲧⲁⲣⲉⲧ⁺] disturb, be disturbed, troubled; m. *disturbance, trouble,*
  confusion

ϣⲧⲟⲩⲏⲧ in ⳁϣⲧⲟⲩⲏⲧ accuse

ϣⲟⲧϣⲧ, ϣⲟⲝⲧ, ϣⲉⲧϣⲱⲧⲉ, ϣⲉⲧϣⲱⲧ⁺ cut, carve; m. *carved object*

ϣⲁⲩ [ϣⲉⲩ], ϣⲟⲩ- m. *use, value*

  ⲣ̅ϣⲁⲩ be useful, prosperous

  ϣⲟⲩ- plus verb *worthy of*

  ϣⲟⲩⲙⲟⲥⲧⲉ fit to be hated

ϣⲁⲩ m. *measure, extent*

ϣⲁⲩ m. *trunk, piece, part*

ϣⲏⲩⲉ f. *altar*

ϣⲟⲟⲩⲉ [ϣⲁⲩⲉⲓⲉ], ϣⲟⲩⲱⲟⲩ⁺ dry up

ϣⲟⲩⲟ, ϣⲟⲩⲉ-, ϣⲟⲩ-, ϣⲟⲩⲱⲉ, ϣⲟⲩⲉⲓⲧ⁺ flow, pour, be empty⁺, vain⁺

ϣⲟⲩⲱⲃⲉ f. *throat*

ϣⲟⲩⲣⲏ f. *censer*

ϣⲟⲩϣⲟⲩ (ⲙ̅ⲙⲟⲉ) pride oneself; ϣⲟⲩϣⲟ m. *boasting, pride*

ϣⲟⲉⲓϣ m. *dust*

ϣⲱϣ, ϣⲟⲩϣⲟⲩ, ϣⲉϣ-, ϣⲁϣⲉ, ϣⲏϣⲉ⁺ scatter, spread

ϣⲱϣ, ϣⲉϣ-, ϣⲁϣⲉ, ϣⲟϣⲉ, ϣⲏϣⲉ⁺ make equal, level, straight; m. *equality,*
  sameness

ϣϣⲉ, ⲉϣϣⲉ, ϣⲉ, ⲥϣⲉ it is suitable, appropriate, necessary
  neg. ⲙⲉϣϣⲉ, ⲙϣϣⲉ it is inappropriate, not fitting

[ϣⲉϣⲧⲉ] v. ⲥⲱϣⲧ stop

ϣⲟϣⲧ [ϣⲁϣⲧ] key v. ⲥⲱϣⲧ

ϣⲟⲩϣⲧ m. *window*

ϣⲟϣⲟⲩ, ϣⲁϣⲟⲩ m. *pot, jar, gallon, measure*

[ϣⲱϣϥ m. *destroyer* (ϩⲱϣϥ)]

ϣⲱϥ, ϣⲉϥ-, ϣⲟϥⲉ, ϣⲏϥⲧ⁺ be desert, waste, destroy; m. *devastation*

ϣϥⲉ, ϣⲃⲉ seventy v. ⲥⲁϣϥ

ϣϥⲱ, ϣⲃⲱ [ϣⲃⲱⲱⲥ] f. *myth, tale*

ϣϥⲧⲉ v. ϣⲓⲃⲉ change

ϣⲱϥⲧ *stumble, err*
  ϣⲁϥⲧⲉ m. *wicked person*
ϣⲁϩ m. *flame, fire*
ϣⲱϩⲃ̄, ϣⲱⲃϩ, ϣⲟϩⲃ⸗, ϣⲟⲃϩ⸗, ϣⲟⲃϩ† *be withered, scorched, wither*
ϣϩⲓⲃ, ϣⲓⲃ m. *dust*
ϣⲁϫⲉ [ϣⲉϫⲉ] *talk, speak, say;* m. *word, saying*
ϣⲱϫⲉ [ⲥⲱϫⲉ] *wrestle;* m. *contest*
  ϣⲟⲉⲓϫ m.f. *athlete*
ϣϫⲉ, pl. ϣϫⲏⲩ m. *locust*
ϣⲟϫⲛⲉ, ϣⲁϫⲛⲉ [ⲥⲁϫⲛⲉ] *take counsel, consider;* m. *counsel, design*
  ϣⲟϫⲛⲉ ⲉ- *make plans about, plot against*
  ϫⲓϣⲟϫⲛⲉ *take counsel, advise*
ϣⲱϫⲡ [ⲥⲱϫⲡ], ϣⲉϫⲡ- [ⲥⲉϫⲡ-], ϣⲟϫⲡ⸗, ϣⲟϫⲡ† *remain over, leave;*
  m. *remainder, rest*
ϣⲟϫⲧ v. ϣⲟⲧϣⲧ *cut*
ϣϫⲓⲧ [ϫϭⲓⲧ] m. *dyer*
[ϣⲱϫϩ, ϣⲁϫϩ⸗, ϣⲁϫⲭ⸗ *diminish*]
ϣⲱⲱϭⲉ, ϣⲟⲟϭ⸗, ϣⲟϭⲉ† *strike, wound*
  ϣϭⲁ m. *blow, wound*
ϣϭⲟⲙ v. ϭⲟⲙ *power*
[ϣϭⲁⲁϭⲉ *be hit;* m. *beat*]

ϥ
called ϥⲁⲓ transliterated *f*

ϥ̄ as number *ninety*
ϥ sometimes interchanges with ⲃ
ϥ- personal pronoun 3rd person sing. masc. *he, it*
-ϥ suffix pronoun 3rd person sing. masc. *him, it*
ϥⲓ, ϥⲉⲓ, ϥⲓ-, ϥⲓⲧ⸗ [ⲃⲓⲧ⸗], ϥⲏⲩ†, p.c. ϥⲁⲓ̈- *carry, lift, take*
  ϥⲓ ⲙⲛ̄- *agree with*
  ϥⲓ ⲛ̄ⲧⲛ̄-, ⲛ̄ⲧⲟⲟⲧ⸗ *take from*
  ϥⲓ ϩⲁ- *bear, endure*
ϥⲱ, ⲃⲱ, ϥⲱⲉ m. *hair*
ϥⲛ̄ⲧ, ⲃⲛ̄ⲧ m.f. *worm*
ϥⲱⲧⲉ, ⲃⲱⲧⲉ, ϥⲉⲧ-, ϥⲟⲧ⸗ *wipe off, obliterate*
  ϥⲱⲧⲉ ⲉⲃⲟⲗ *wipe out, destroy;* m. *destruction*
ϥⲱⲧⲉ v. ⲃⲱⲧⲉ *pollute*
ϥⲧⲟⲟⲩ [ϥⲧⲁⲩ], f. ϥⲧⲟⲉ, ϥⲧⲟ, ϥⲧⲟⲩ-, ϥⲧⲉⲩ-, -ⲁϥⲧⲉ *four*
[ϥⲟⲩϩⲉ v. ⲃⲟⲩϩⲉ *eyelid*]
ϥⲱϭⲉ, ⲃⲱϭⲉ, ϥⲉϭ-, ϥⲟϭ⸗ *jump, rush, seize, rob*
  ϥⲱϭⲥ, ⲃⲱϭⲥ *jump, rush*
  ϥⲟϭⲥ, ⲃⲟϭⲥ in ϫⲓϥⲟϭⲥ *hop, dance*

ⲍ

called ⲍⲟⲡⲓ   transliterated *h*

ⲍ   for Gk. rough breathing

[ⲍⲁ- indicates apposition]

ⲍⲁ-, ⲍⲁⲡⲟ⸗   *under, in, at, from, for, for the sake of, concerning, against*
    ⲍⲁⲡⲓⲍⲁⲡⲟ⸗   *-self, alone*

ⲍⲁ   m. *winnowing fan*

ⲍⲁⲉ, f. ⲍⲁⲏ, pl. ⲍⲁⲉⲉⲩ, ⲍⲁⲉⲟⲩ   m. *last, end*
    ⲉⲡⲍⲁⲉ, ⲉⲑⲁⲏ   *at the end, finally*
    ⲡ̄ⲍⲁⲉ   *be last, be in want, need*

ⲍⲁⲓ̈ [ⲍⲉⲉⲓ]   m. *husband*

ⲍⲁⲓ̈ⲟ, ⲁⲓ̈ⲱ   *hey!, hail!*

ⲍⲉ [ⲍⲁⲉⲓⲉ], ⲍⲏⲩ†   *fall, be falling†; m. fall, destruction*
    ⲍⲉ ⲉ-   *find, discover*
    ⲍⲉ ⲉⲃⲟⲗ   *perish*

ⲍⲉ, ⲍⲓⲏ [ⲍⲉⲉⲥ]   f. *way, manner*
    ⲛ̄ⲑⲉ ⲛ̄-   *in the way of, like, as*
    ⲛ̄ⲧⲉⲓ̈ⲍⲉ [ⲛ̄†ⲍⲉ]   *thus, so*
    ⲛ̄ⲧⲉⲓ̈ⲍⲉ ⲧⲏⲣⲥ   *so much*
    ⲛ̄ⲁⲱ ⲛ̄ⲍⲉ   *how?*
    ⲕⲁⲧⲁ ⲑⲉ   *like (κατά)*
    ⲡ̄ⲑⲉ ⲛ̄-   *become like*
    † ⲑⲉ   *enable*
    ⲧⲁⲓ̈ ⲧⲉ ⲑⲉ   *so it is, thus*

ⲍⲉ v. ⲉⲍⲉ   *yes*

ⲍⲉ-   m. *time, season*
    ⲍⲉⲃⲱⲱⲛ   m. *famine*
    ⲍⲉⲛⲟⲩⳓⲉ   m. *plenty*

ⲍⲏ, ⲍⲓⲏ, ⲉⲍⲏ, ⲍⲏⲧ⸗, ⲉⲍⲏⲧ⸗   f. *front, beginning*
    ⲍⲏⲧ⸗   *come, go, look, etc. forward, fear, etc. before*
    ⲉⲑⲏ   *forward*
    ⲛ̄ⲥⲁⲑⲏ   *in front, formerly, from now on*
    ⲍⲁⲑⲏ, ⲍⲁⲧⲉ⸗ ⲍⲏ   *in front, before*
    ⲍⲓⲑⲏ, ⲍⲓⲍⲏ   *to, in front, before*

ⲍⲏ, ⲍⲏⲧ⸗   f. *belly, womb*
    ⲛ̄ⲍⲏⲧ⸗   *in used as the presuffixal form of ⲍⲛ̄-, q.v.*

ⲍⲏ, ⲍⲉ   f. *story of a house*

ⲍⲓ, ⲍⲓⲧ⸗, ⲍⲁⲧ⸗   *thresh, beat, rub*

ⲍⲓ- v. ⲍⲓⲟⲩⲉ   *hit*

ⲍⲓ-, ⲍⲓⲱⲱ⸗   *upon, on, at, in, concerning, from, in time of, and, or*
    ⲍⲓⲱⲧ-   with ⲧⲏⲩⲧⲛ̄
    ⲍⲓⲛⲁⲓ̈   *thus*

ⲍⲓⲉ, ⲍⲓⲏ, pl. ⲍⲓⲏⲩ v. ⲍⲓⲛⲓⲉ   *rudder*

[ⲍⲓ̈ⲉ] v. ⲉⲓ̈ⲉ   *then*

ⲍⲓⲏ, pl. ⲍⲓⲟⲟⲩⲉ   f. *road, way*

ⲍⲟ, ⲍⲱ, ⲍⲣⲁ⸗ [ⲍⲣⲉ⸗]   m. *face*
    ϫⲓⲍⲟ   *respect, pay attention*
    ϫⲓⲍⲣⲁ⸗   *occupy oneself, converse; m. distraction*

[ⲧⲍⲟ *encourage;* m. *exhortation*]

ⲍⲁⲗⲍⲟ m. *deceiving face*

ⲉⲍⲣⲛ-, ⲉⲍⲣⲁⲍ [ⲁⲍⲣⲉⲍ] *to, among*

ⲛⲁⲍⲣⲛ- [ⲛⲛⲁⲍⲣⲛ-], ⲛⲁⲍⲣⲁⲍ [ⲛⲛⲁⲍⲣⲁⲍ, ⲛⲁⲍⲣⲉⲍ] *before, compared with*

ⲍⲟⲓ m. *field, water-wheel*

ⲍⲟⲓ in ⲧⲍⲟⲓ *take the trouble*

ⲍⲱ (ⲉⲣⲟⲍ) *be enough, satisfy*

ⲍⲱ ⲉⲣⲟⲍ ⲉ- *be satisfied with*

ⲍⲱⲱⲍ, ⲍⲱⲍ *-self, also, too, even*

ⲍⲱ *I too, even I*

ⲍⲱⲧ- with ⲑⲏⲧⲛ

ⲍⲱⲱϥ *but, on the other hand*

ⲍⲓⲉⲓⲃ m.f. *lamb*

ⲍⲱⲃ, ⲍⲱϥ, pl. ⲍⲃⲏⲩⲉ m. *thing, work, event, deed*

ⲟⲩ ⲡⲉ ⲡⲍⲱⲃ *what is the matter?*

ⲣ̄ⲍⲱⲃ *work*

ϣⲃⲣ̄ⲣ̄ⲍⲱⲃ m. *fellow worker*

ⲍⲏⲃⲉ m.f. *grief, mourning*

ⲣ̄ⲍⲏⲃⲉ *grieve, mourn*

ⲍⲓⲃⲉ, ⲍⲟⲃⲉⲧ *be low, short*

ⲍⲃ̄ⲃⲉ m. *low part*

ⲍⲃⲁ m. *embarrassment, misfortune*

ⲣ̄ⲍⲃⲁ *be in distress*

ⲍⲃⲱ f. *covering, tent*

ⲍⲃ̄ⲃⲉ, ⲍⲏⲩⲃⲉ m. *plow*

ⲍⲃⲟⲩⲣ [ϭⲃⲟⲩⲣ] f. *left hand, left*

ⲍⲃⲟⲣⲃⲣ̄ [ⲍⲃⲁⲣⲃⲣ̄] *push, throw*

[ⲍⲓⲉⲃⲣⲏⲭ, ⲍⲃⲃⲣⲏϭⲉ] v. ⲉⲃⲣⲏϭⲉ *lightning*

ⲍⲁⲓⲃⲉⲥ, ⲍⲟⲓⲃⲉⲥ [ⲍⲁⲉⲓⲃⲉ] f. *shadow*

ⲍⲏⲃⲥ, ⲍⲃ̄ⲥ m. *lamp*

ⲍⲱⲃⲥ, ⲍⲱⲃⲉⲥ, ⲍⲃⲥ-, ⲍⲟⲃⲥⲍ [ⲍⲟϥⲥⲍ], ⲍⲟⲃⲥⲧ [ⲍⲁⲃⲥⲧ] *cover, be covered*

ⲍⲱⲃⲥ, ⲍⲟⲃⲥ, ⲍⲃ̄ⲥ m. *covering, lid*

ⲍⲃⲟⲟⲥ, ⲍⲃⲟⲥ, pl. ⲍⲃⲱⲱⲥ m.f. *garment, linen*

ⲍⲃ̄ⲥⲱ [ⲍⲃ̄ⲥⲟⲩ], pl. ⲍⲃ̄ⲥⲟⲟⲩⲉ f. *garment*

ⲍⲃⲏⲧⲉ v. ⲥⲍⲃⲏⲏⲧⲉ *foam*

ⲍⲁⲃⲁϭⲏⲉⲓⲛ v. ⲁⲃⲁϭⲏⲉⲓⲛ *glass*

ⲍⲁⲕ *sober, prudent*

ⲍⲓⲕ m. *magic*

ⲍⲱⲕ, ⲍⲉⲕ-, ⲍⲟⲕⲍ, ⲍⲏⲕⲧ *gird, arm, brace;* m. *belt, breastplate*

ⲍⲁⲕⲟ m. *magician*

ⲍⲱⲱⲕⲉ, ⲍⲱⲕⲉ, ⲍⲟⲟⲕⲉⲧ *scrape, scratch, shave*

ⲍⲕⲟ, ⲍⲕⲁⲉⲓⲧⲧ *be hungry;* m. *hunger, famine*

ⲍⲏⲕⲉ m.f. *poor person, poor*

ⲙⲛ̄ⲧⲍⲏⲕⲉ f. *poverty*

ⲍⲱⲕⲙ̄ v. ⲍⲱϭⲃ̄ *wither*

ⲍⲁⲗ in ⲣ̄ⲍⲁⲗ *deceive*

ⲍⲁⲗ m.f. *servant, slave*

ⲍⲙ̄ⲍⲁⲗ, ⲍⲙ̄ⲍⲉⲗ m.f. *servant, slave*

ⲣ̄ⲍⲙ̄ⲍⲁⲗ *serve, be enslaved*

ϢⲂⲢϨⲘϨⲀⲖ   m.f. *fellow servant*
ϨⲰⲖ, ϨⲎⲀ†   *fly*
ϨⲞⲞⲖⲈ   f. *moth*
ϨⲰⲰⲖⲈ, ϨⲰⲖⲈ, ϨⲀⲖ-, ϨⲞⲖ⸍   *pluck, tear*
[ϨⲀⲈⲒ   *anyone, anything, no one, nothing*]
ϨⲰⲀⲔ   *twist, braid*; m. *braid*
ϨⲖ̄ⲖⲞ, f. ϨⲖ̄ⲖⲰ, pl. ϨⲖ̄ⲖⲞ̈   m. *old man, elder, old*, f. *old woman* (ϨⲀⲖ plus -Ⲟ)
[ϨⲀⲀⲘⲈ, ϨⲀⲀⲘⲎ   f. *spring, fountain*]
ϨⲖⲞⲘⲖⲘ̄, [ϨⲀⲎⲘ†]   *be complicated, entangled*; m. *complication*
ϨⲖ̄ⲡⲈ [ϨⲞⲖⲡⲈ]   f. *navel*
ϨⲖⲞⲤⲦⲚ̄   m. *mist, fog*
ϨⲀⲖⲎⲦ, pl. ϨⲀⲖⲀⲦⲈ   m. *bird* (ϨⲰⲖ)
[ϨⲀⲖϨⲖ̄, ϨⲖ̄ϨⲰⲖ⸍   *kill, slay*]
ϨⲖⲞϬ [ϨⲀⲖϬ], ϨⲞⲖϬ† [ϨⲀⲖⲈϬ†]   *be sweet, delighted*; m. *sweetness*
     ϨⲖ̄ϬⲈ   m.f. *sweetness*
ϨⲀⲘ, ϨⲀⲘ-, ϨⲘ̄-, pl. ϨⲘⲎⲨ   m. *craftsman, worker*
     ϨⲀⲘⲚⲞⲨⲂ   m. *goldsmith*
     ϨⲀⲘϢⲈ   m. *carpenter*
ϨⲞⲈⲒⲘ, pl. ϨⲎⲘⲈ   m. *wave*
ϨⲰⲘ, ϨⲈⲘ-, ϨⲞⲘ⸍, ϨⲎⲘ†   *tread, trample*
ϨⲀⲘⲞ̈ [ϨⲀⲘⲀⲈⲒ]   *would that, oh that*
ϨⲒⲘⲈ, pl. ϨⲒⲞⲘⲈ   f. *wife*
ϨⲒⲞⲘⲈ [ϨⲒⲀⲘⲈ]   *women* v. ⲤϨⲒⲘⲈ
ϨⲒⲰⲘⲈ, ϨⲰⲘⲈ   f. *palm* of the hand
ϨⲘⲈ   *forty*
ϨⲘⲞⲨ   m. *salt*
ϨⲘⲞⲘ, ϨⲎⲘ†   *be hot*; m. *heat, fever*
     ϨⲘ̄ⲘⲈ   f. *heat, fever*
ϨⲘ̄ⲘⲈ in Ⲣ̄ϨⲘ̄ⲘⲈ   *steer, guide*
ϨⲘⲈⲚⲈ   *eighty* v. ϢⲘⲞⲨⲚ
ϨⲞⲘⲚ̄Ⲧ, ϨⲞⲘⲦ   m. *copper, bronze, money*
ϨⲀⲘⲎⲢ   m. *arms, embrace*
ϨⲘ̄Ⲥ   m. *spike of wheat*
ϨⲘⲞⲞⲤ† [ϨⲘⲀⲤⲦ†]   *sit, dwell*
     ϨⲘⲞⲞⲤ ⲘⲚ̄-   *marry*
     ⲘⲀ Ⲛ̄ϨⲘⲞⲞⲤ   m. *seat, throne, toilet, anus*
ϨⲘⲞⲦ [ϨⲘⲀⲦ]   m. *grace, gift*
     ϢⲠϨⲘⲞⲦ   *give thanks* (ϢⲰⲠ *receive*)
ϨⲘ̄ϨⲀⲖ v. ϨⲀⲖ   *servant*
ϨⲘ̄ϨⲘ̄   *roar*
ϨⲘ̄ⲞⲖ, ϨⲞⲘ⳥†   *be sour*
     ϨⲘ̄ⳤ   m. *vinegar*
ϨⲚ̄-, Ⲛ̄ϨⲎⲦ⸍   *in, at, on, by, from, among*
     [ϨⲚ̄Ⲛ-   before vowels especially the indef. art. sing.]
     ⲈⲂⲞⲖ ϨⲚ̄-   *from*
     ϨⲚ̄ⲞⲨ-   forms adverbs of manner
     The paradigm for Ⲛ̄ϨⲎⲦ⸍ and other presuffixal forms ending in a
     consonant is this:
     Ⲛ̄ϨⲎⲦ   *in me*

N̄2HTK   *in you* sing. masc.
N̄2HTE   *in you* sing. fem.
N̄2HTY   *in him*
N̄2HTC   *in her*
N̄2HTN̄   *in us*
N̄2HTTHYTN̄   *in you* pl.
N̄2HTOY   *in them*
2EN- [2N̄-]   indefinite article pl. *some* (2OEINE)
2OYN   m. *interior, inside*
    2N̄-   q.v., *in*
    E2OYN [λ2OYN]   *to, toward, inward*
    E2OYN E-, EPO⳽   *into*
    N̄2OYN   *within*
    M̄ΦOYN N̄-   *within*
    2I2OYN   *within*
2WN [2NλN], 2N̄-, 2ON⳽, 2HN†   *approach, be near*†
2WN, 2ON⳽ (ETOOT⳽)   *command*
2WN   *go aground*
    O N̄2WN   *be shallow*
2HNE   m. *spice, incense*
    (ϢOY2HNE   m. *incense*
2INE (EBOλ)   *row out*
2INE, 2N̄T⳽   *move oneself*
    2N̄T⳽ EBOλ   *remove oneself*
2INIE, 2IE, 2IH, pl. 2IHY   m. *rudder*
2OEINE [2λEINE, 2OEIN], 2EN- [2N̄-]   *some, certain*
2NE-, E2NE-, 2Nλ⳽ [2NE⳽], E2Nλ⳽ [E2NE⳽]   *be willing, pleased, glad* (subj.
    as suffix)
    P̄2Nλ⳽   *desire, want, be willing*
2INHB, 2INHY   *sleep;* m. *sleep*
2ONBE   f. *spring, well*
[2WNT, 2λNT†   *approach, be near*†, *at hand*†, *fate*†]
2ENEETE   f. *monastery, convent*
2NλλY   m. *pot, jar, thing*
[2NW2E   f. *fear*]
2λΠ [2EΠ]   m. *judgment, justice*
    †2λΠ   *judge*
2WΠ, 2EΠ-, 2OΠ⳽ [2λΠ⳽], 2HΠ†   *hide, be hidden, be secret*†
2λΠC [2λΨ]   *it is necessary*
2ΠOT, 2ΠWT   n. *fathom*
2IΠ   m. *street*
2WP   *Horus,* name of fourth-century monk
2Pλ⳽ v. 2O   *face*
2Pλ⳽ v. 2POOY   *voice*
2λPO⳽ v. 2λ-   *under*
2λPW⳽   *beneath, before* v. PO
2IPW⳽   *at, upon* v. PO
2Pλï [2PHï, 2PE]   m. *upper part, lower part*
    E2Pλï [λ2PHï]   *upward, downward*

ϨΡⲀⲒ [ⲚϨΡⲀⲒ] ϨⲚ-, ⲚϨΗΤ⸗ *in, within*
ϨⲢⲉ, pl. ϨⲢΗⲨⲉ f. *food*
   ϨⲢⲉⲂⲞⲦ *per month*
ϨⲢⲰ f. *oven, furnace*
ϨⲢⲂ̄ m. *form, likeness*
ϨⲰⲢⲂ̄, ϨⲞⲢⲂ⸗ *be broken, break*
ϨⲢⲂⲰⲦ f. *staff, rod*
ϨⲢⲞⲔ, ϨⲢΗϬ, ϨⲞⲢⲔ† *be still, quiet, stop*
   †ϨⲢⲞⲔ [ⲐⲢⲔⲞ] *calm, subdue*
ϨⲢⲘⲀⲚ [ⲀⲀϨⲘⲉⲚ] m. *pomegranate*
ϨⲀⲢⲚ̄- *beneath, before* v. ⲢⲞ
ϨⲒⲢⲚ̄- *at, upon* v. ⲢⲞ
ϨⲰⲢⲠ, ϨⲉⲢⲠ-, ϨⲞⲢⲠ⸗, ϨⲞⲢⲠ† *be wet, drench, soak*
ϨⲢΗⲢⲉ m. *flower*
ϨⲀⲢⲀⲦ⸗ *beneath* v. ⲢⲀⲦ⸗
ϨⲢⲰⲦ f. *wine-press, vat*
[ϨⲢ̄Ⲧⲉ f. *fear*]
ϨⲢⲞⲞⲨ [ϨⲢⲀⲞⲨ, ϨⲢⲀⲨ], ϨⲢⲞⲨ-, ϨⲢⲀ⸗ m. *voice, sound, noise*
   ϨⲢⲞⲨⲘ̄Ⲡⲉ m. *thunder*
   ϨⲢⲞⲨⲂⲂⲀⲒ̈ f. *thunder*
   ⲘⲚ̄ⲦϨⲢⲞⲨⲞ f. *boastfulness* (-ⲟ)
ϨⲢⲞϢ [ϨⲢⲀϢ], ϨⲞⲢϢ† [ϨⲀⲢϢ†], p.c. ϨⲀⲢϢ- *be heavy, slow, make heavy, burden;* m. *weight, burden*
   ⲘⲚ̄ⲦϨⲀⲢϢϨΗⲦ f. *patience*
   ϨⲢΗϢⲉ f. *weight*
ϨⲀⲢⲉϨ, ⲀⲢⲉϨ, ⲉⲢⲉϨ [ⲀⲢΗϨ] *keep, guard*
ϨⲢⲰϪⲉ n. *boundary*
ϨⲢⲞϪⲢϪ *grind* (teeth)
[ϨⲀⲤ⸗] v. ⲰϨⲤ *reap*
[ϨⲉⲉⲤ] v. Ϩⲉ *way*
ϨⲰⲤ *sing;* m. *song, hymn*
ϨⲰⲤ, ϨⲉⲤ-, ϨⲀⲤ⸗ *block, obstruct, fill*
ϨⲀⲤⲒⲉ m. *drowned person*
   Ϣⲉ Ⲛ̄ϨⲀⲤⲒⲉ *be drowned, shipwrecked*
ϨⲒⲤⲉ, ϨⲀⲤⲦ⸗, ϨⲞⲤⲉ†, [ϨⲀⲤⲒ†] *work, be bothered, be difficult, be tired, trouble oneself;* m. *labor, weariness, suffering*
   ϢⲠϨⲒⲤⲉ *labor, suffer*
ϨⲒⲤⲉ, ϨⲒⲤⲦ⸗, ϨⲞⲤⲉ† *spin*
ϨⲞⲤⲂ̄ f. *market*
ϨⲀⲦ, ϨⲀⲦⲉ m. *silver, money*
ϨⲀⲉⲒⲦ f. *porch, forecourt*
ϨΗⲦ, ϨⲦΗ⸗, [pl. ϨⲉⲦⲉ] m. *heart, mind*
   Ϥ̄ϨΗⲦ ⲤⲚⲀⲨ *doubt, hesitate*
   ⲀⲦϨΗⲦ, ⲀⲐΗⲦ *senseless, ignorant, foolish*
   ⲂⲀⲀϨΗⲦ *simple-minded, harmless*
   ⲢⲘ̄Ⲛ̄ϨΗⲦ n. *wise person*
   ⲘⲚ̄ⲦⲢⲘ̄Ⲛ̄ϨΗⲦ f. *understanding, intelligence*
   ϢⲤⲚ̄ϨΗⲦ m. *grief*
   ⲔⲰ Ⲛ̄ϨΗⲦ, ⲔⲀϨⲦΗ⸗ ⲉ- *trust*

ₚ₂ΤΗˊ *reflect, regret*

†₂ΤΗˊ *observe, consider, pay attention*

ϣₙ₂ΤΗˊ, ϣΑΝ₂ΤΗˊ *have pity, compassion* (ϣωΝΕ)

ΜΝ̄Τϣₙ₂ΤΗϥ f. *mercy*

₂Α₂Τₙ̄-, ₂Α(₂)ΤΕ-, ₂Α(₂)ΤΗˊ *with, beside*

₂ΗΤ m. *north*

₂ΗΤ, ₂ΤΗˊ m. *tip, edge*

₂ΗΤˊ v. ₂Η and ₂ₙ̄-

₂ΙΤˊ v. ₂Ι *thresh*

₂ΙΤˊ v. ₂ΙΟΥΕ *hit*

₂ΙΕΙΤ m. *pit*

₂ωΤ, ₂ΟΤ m. *sack, bag*

₂ωΤ in ₚ₂ωΤ *sail*

₂ΑΤΕ, ₂ΑΑΤΕ [₂Ε†Ε, ₂†Ε] *flow, pour*

₂ΙΤΕ, ₂ΕΤ-, ₂ΑΤˊ *move around, rub, be worn out, be convulsed*

₂ΟΕΙΤΕ m.f. *garment, cloak*

₂ΟΕΙΤΕ f. *hyena*

₂ΟΤΕ [₂Α†Ε] f. *fear*

   ₚ₂ΟΤΕ ₂ΗΤˊ *be afraid of, fear*

₂ΤΟ, Ε₂ΤΟ, pl. ₂ΤωωΡ m. *horse*

₂ωΤΒ̄ [₂ωΤΒΕ], ₂ΕΤΒ̄-, ₂ΟΤΒˊ, ₂ΟΤΒ̄†, p.c. ₂ΑΤΒ̄- *kill;* m. *murder*

   ₂ΑΤΒΕС [₂ΕΤΒΕ, ₂ΑΤΒΕ] f. *slaughter, corpse*

₂ΤΟΜΤΜ̄ [₂ωΤΜ̄, ₂ΤΜ̄ΤΜ̄, ₂ΤΟΜ₂ΤΜ̄], ₂ΤΜ̄Τωμ† *be darkened, darken,*
   extinguish; m. *darkness*

₂ΑΤₙ̄-, ₂ΑΤΟΟΤˊ *with* v. ΤωΡΕ

₂ΙΤₙ̄, ₂ΙΤΟΟΤˊ *through* v. ΤωΡΕ

₂ωΤΠ [₂ωΤϥ], ₂ΕΤΠ-, ₂ΟΤΠˊ, ₂ΟΤΠ† *join, be reconciled, set (sun, stars);*
   m. *reconciliation, bond*

   ΜΑ Ν̄₂ωΤΠ, СΑ Ν̄₂ωΤΠ n. *west*

₂ωΤₚ [₂ωΤΡΕ], ₂ΕΤΡ-, ₂ΟΤΡˊ, ₂ΟΤΡ† [₂ΑΤΡΕ†] *be joined, doubled, join,*
   hire; m. *joint, union*

   [ϣΒₚΝ̄₂ωΤΡ m. *consort, syzygos*]

   ₂ΑΤΡΕ, pl. ₂ΑΤΡΕΕΥ m. *twin*

₂ΤΟΡ m. *necessity, constraint*

₂ΑΤΗΥ *whirlwind* v. ΤΗΥ

₂ΤΟΟΥΕ f. *dawn, morning*

₂ΙΤΟΥΝ-, ₂ΙΤΟΥωˊ *beside* v. ΤΟΥωˊ

₂ΑΘωΡ *name of 3rd Egyptian month (Hathor)*

₂ΟΤ₂Τ, ₂ΕΤ₂Τ-, ₂ΕΤ₂ωΤˊ, ₂ΕΤ₂ωΤ† *ask, inquire, examine;* m. *question*

₂ΗΥ, ₂ΗΟΥ m. *profit, usefulness*

   †₂ΗΥ *give profit, benefit, gain*

   6Ν̄₂ΗΥ *find profit, gain*

₂ΟΟΥ [₂ωΟΥ] m. *day*

   ΠΟΟΥ, Μ̄ΠΟΟΥ *today*

   ΠΟΟΥ Ν̄₂ΟΟΥ *this day*

₂ΟΟΥₚ [₂ΑΥ†, ₂ΑΟΥ†, ₂ΑΥΟΥ†] *be bad†, wicked†, evil†*

   ΠΕΘΟΟΥ m. *evil, wickedness (substantive, can take def. art.* ΠΠΕΘΟΟΥ)

₂ωΟΥ, ₂ΟΥ- *rain;* m. *rain, moisture*

   ΜΟΥΝ̄₂ωΟΥ m. *rain*

ϨΙΟΥⲈ, ϨΙ-, ϨΙΤ⳹ *hit, beat, throw*
  ϨΙΤΟΟΤ⳹ *undertake, attempt, begin*
ϨΙΟΟΥⲈ *roads* v. ϨΙΗ
ϨΟΥΟ, ϨΟΥⲈ- m. *greater part, greatness, excess, much, more, most*
  ϨΟΥΟ Ⲉ- *beyond, more than*
  ⲈϨΟΥΟ Ⲉ-, ⲈϨΟΥⲈ-, ⲈϨΟΥⲈΡΟ⳹ *more than, rather than*
  ⲈⲠⲈϨΟΥΟ *greatly, very*
  Ⲛ̄ϨΟΥΟ *greatly, rather, more, very*
  Ⲣ̄ϨΟΥΟ *exceed, be more, be abundant*
ϨΟΥΡⲈ-, ϨΟΥΡⲰ⳹ [ϨΟΥΡΟⲈΙΤ†] *deprive*
ϨΟΥΡΙΤ, pl. ϨΟΥΡⲀΤⲈ m. *watchman, guardian*
ϨΟΥⲈΙΤ, f. ϨΟΥⲈΙΤⲈ, pl. ϨΟΥⲀΤⲈ n. *first,* f. *beginning*
ϨΟΟΥΤ [ϨⲀΥΤ], ϨΟΥΤ- m. *male, husband, wild* man or plant
  [ϨΟΥΤⲤϨΙΜⲈ *androgyne*]
ϨΟΟΥΤⲚ̄ m. *road, highway*
ϨΟΟΥϢ *insult, curse*
ϨΟΥϨⲈ [ΟΥϨⲈ, ϨΟΥⲈ] m. *miscarriage, abortion*
ϨⲀΥϬⲀⲖ m. *anchor, hook*
ϨⲰϢ, ϨⲈϢ-, ϨΗϢ† *be in distress, torment;* m. *distress torment*
[ϨⲰϢϥ, ϨΟϢϥ⳹, ϨⲀϢϥ⳹ *break*]
ϨΟϥ [ϨⲀϥ], f. ϨϥⲰ, ϨΒⲰ, pl. ϨΒΟΥΙ m.f. *serpent, snake*
ϨⲰϥΤ, ϨⲈϥΤ-, ϨΟϥΤ⳹ *steal*
ϨⲀϨ n. *many, much*
ϨⲰϨ, ϨΟϨ⳹ *be scraped, itch, scrape, scratch*
ϨⲀϨΤⲚ̄-, ϨⲀϨΤⲈ-, ϨⲀϨΤΗ⳹ *with* v. ϨΗΤ
ϨⲰϪ, ϨⲈϪ-, ϨΗϪ† *be constrained, constrict*
ϨΙϪⲚ̄-, ϨΙϪⲰ⳹ *upon* v. ϪⲰ⳹
ϨϪΟⲠϪⲠ v. ϪΟⲠϪⲠ *grope*
ϨΟϪϨϪ, ϨΟϪϪ, ϨⲈϪϨⲰϪ† [ϨϬⲀϬΤ†] *be restrained, narrow, compel;*
  m. *distress*
ϨⲰϬⲂ, ϨⲰⲔⲘ̄, ϨⲈϬⲂ-, ϨΟϬⲂ⳹, ϨΟϬⲂ† *wither, expire, fade*
ϨⲰϬⲂ, ϨΟϬⲂ†, [ϨΟϬⲂⲈⲤ] v. ϬⲂⲂ *be cold*
ϨⲀϬΙⲚ m. *mint*

Ϫ
called ϪⲀⲚϪΙⲀ transliterated *j*

ϪⲀⲒⲈ, ϪⲀⲈ m. *desert, wilderness*
ϪⲀⲒΟ [ϪⲀⲈΙⲀ⳹] v. ΤϪⲀⲒΟ *triumph*
ϪⲈ- *namely, that, because, for*
  introduces a quotation " . . . "
  with III future [II future] *so that . . . might*
  ϪⲈⲚⲈ- *if, whether* (ϪⲈ- ⲈⲚⲈ-)
  ⲈⲂΟⲖ ϪⲈ- *because*
ϪΗ f. *dish, bowl*
ϪΗ m. *chip, speck*
  ϪΙⲚϪΗ m. *emptiness, nothing* (chip of a chip)
  ⲈⲠϪΙⲚϪΗ *in vain, for no reason*

ϫι, ϫει, ϫι-, ϫει-, ϫιτ⸍, ϫηγ†, p.c. ϫαï-, ϫαγ- *receive, take, get;* m. *theft*
  ϫι ε- *lead, attain to*
  ϫι- forms compound infinitives such as:
  ϫιμοειτ *lead, guide*
  ϫιϯ *trade*
  ϫιϯπε *taste*
ϫο, ϫω, ϫε-, ϫο⸍, ϫηγ† *sow, plant;* m. *sowing*
  ϫο, ϫε-, ϫο⸍ *put, spend, send forth*
ϫο m. *armpit*
ϫοε, ϫοï, ϫο, pl. εϫη f. *wall*
  ϫενετμητε f. *middle wall*
ϫοï, pl. εϫηγ m. *ship, boat*
ϫω [ϫογ], ϫε-, ϫι-, ϫοο⸍, imper. ⲁϫι-, ⲁϫι⸍, p.c. ϫⲁⲧ- *say, speak, tell, sing*
  ϫω ⲙ̄ⲙⲟⲥ ϫε-, ϫⲟⲟⲥ ϫε- *say* " ... "
  ϫερο⸍ *say to, mean* (ϫω ⲉⲣⲟ⸍)
ϫω⸍ *head of* (ϫωϫ, in compounds, cf. ⲁⲡⲉ)
  ⲉϫⲛ̄- [ⲁϫⲛ̄-], ⲉϫⲱ⸍ [ⲁϫⲱ⸍] *upon, onto, over, for, to, against, on account of, after*
  ϩⲓϫⲛ̄-, ϩⲓϫⲱ⸍ *upon, over*
ϫω m. *cup*
ϫⲱⲱⲃⲉ [ϫⲱⲃⲉ], ϫⲟⲟⲃ⸍ *pass through, by*
[ϫⲃ̄ⲃⲓⲱ] *substitution* v. ϣⲓⲃⲉ
ϫⲃ̄ⲃⲉⲥ m.f. *coal*
ϫⲱⲕ, ϫⲉⲕ-, ϫⲟⲕ⸍ [ϫⲁⲕ⸍], ϫⲏⲕ† (ⲉⲃⲟⲗ) *fill, finish, be completed, be full†, complete†, perfect†;* m. *end, total, perfection*
ϫⲱⲱⲕⲉ, ϫⲟⲟⲕ⸍ *sting*
ϫⲱⲕⲙ̄, ϫⲉⲕⲙ-, ϫⲟⲕⲙ⸍, ϫⲟⲕⲙ̄† *wash, baptize;* m. *washing, baptism*
ϫⲱⲕⲣ̄, ϫⲉⲕⲣ-, ϫⲟⲕⲣ⸍, ϫⲟⲕⲣ̄† *salt, season*
ϫⲉⲕⲁⲁⲥ, ϫⲉⲕⲁⲥ [ϫⲉⲕⲁⲥⲉ] *in order that, so that* (ϫⲉ- ⲕⲁⲁ⸍)
ϫⲱⲕϫⲕ *prick, brand;* m. *provocation*
ϫⲱ(ⲱ)ⲗⲉ, ϫⲉⲗⲉ-, ϫⲟⲗ⸍ *gather, harvest;* m. *harvest*
ϫⲱⲗⲕ, ϫⲉⲗⲕ- [ϫⲁϭ-], ϫⲟⲗⲕ⸍, ϫⲟⲗⲕ† *stretch, sew*
[ϫⲱⲗⲕ, ϫⲁⲗⲕ⸍ *be submerged*
  ⲣⲉϥϫⲁⲗⲕ- m. *one submerged in*]
ϫⲟⲟⲗⲉⲥ f. *moth*
ϫⲟⲗϩ† *be smallest†, least†*
ϫⲟⲗϫⲝ̄ *fence in;* m. *hedge, fence*
ϫⲱⲗϭ v. ϭⲟⲗϫ *entangle*
ϫⲱⲙ [ϫⲱⲱⲙⲉ] m. *generation*
ϫⲁⲙⲏ f. *calm*
ϫⲱⲱⲙⲉ, ϫⲱⲙⲉ [ϫⲁⲙⲉ, pl. ϫⲙⲉ] m. *book, papyrus sheet* or *roll*
ϫⲛ̄-, ϫⲉⲛ-, ϫⲓⲛ-, ϫⲉ- *or*
  ϫⲛ̄ⲙ̄ⲙⲟⲛ, ϫⲉⲙ̄ⲙⲟⲛ *or not*
ϫⲓⲛ-, ϫⲛ̄- *from, since*
  ϫⲓⲛⲧⲁ⸍ (with II perfect) *while, since*
[ϫⲓⲛ m. *power*]
ϫⲛⲁ, ϫⲛⲉ, ϫⲛⲉ- [ϫⲉⲛⲉ-], ϫⲛⲁ⸍, ϫⲉⲛⲁ⸍ *send, hit, beat, extinguish* (caus. of ϣⲉ)

ⲝⲉⲛⲉ- *if* v. ⲝⲉ-

ⲝⲛⲟⲩ, ⲝⲛⲉ-, ⲝⲛ̄-, ⲝⲛⲟⲩ⸗ *ask, inquire, question, tell, say* (ϣⲟⲝⲛⲉ)

ⲝⲉⲛⲉⲡⲱⲣ f. *roof*

ⲝⲱⲛⲧ, ⲝⲛ̄ⲧ-, ⲝⲁⲛⲧ⸗, ⲝⲟⲛⲧ† *try, test, begin*

ⲝⲛⲁⲁⲩ, ⲝⲛⲁⲩ *delay*

ⲝⲛⲟⲟⲩ m. *threshing floor*

ⲝⲱⲛϥ, ⲝⲟⲟⲛⲉϥ† *happen, meet with*; m. *chance, agreement*

ⲝⲛⲟϥ m. *basket, crate*

ⲝⲛⲁϩ m. *forearm, strength, violence*

ⲝⲓⲛⲝⲏ *emptiness* v. ⲝⲏ

ⲝⲡ- f. *hour* (prefixed to a cardinal number)

ⲝⲡⲓ-, ⲝⲡⲉ- *must* (followed by an infinitive)

ⲝⲡⲓⲟ, ⲝⲡⲓⲉ-, ⲝⲡⲓⲟ⸗, ⲝⲡⲓⲏⲧ† *blame, convict* (caus. of ϣⲓⲡⲉ)

ⲝⲡⲟ, ⲝⲡⲉ-, ⲝⲡⲟ⸗ [ⲝⲡⲁ⸗] *give birth to, produce, acquire*; m. *birth, one born* (caus. of ϣⲱⲡⲉ)

 [ⲁⲧⲝⲡⲟ⸗ *unbegotten*]

ⲝⲟⲡⲝⲡ, ϩⲝⲟⲡⲝⲡ *grope,* [*tread*]

ⲝⲏⲣ *be cheerful, have fun*; m. *joke, play*

ⲝⲱⲣ, ⲝⲟⲟⲣ⸗ *examine*; m. *spy*

ⲝⲉⲣⲟ, ⲝⲉⲣⲱ, ⲝⲉⲣⲉ-, ⲝⲉⲣⲟ⸗, ⲝⲉⲣⲱ⸗ *burn, ignite*

ⲝⲱⲱⲣⲉ, ⲝⲱⲣⲉ [ⲝⲱⲱⲣ], ⲝⲉⲣⲉ-, ⲝⲟⲟⲣ⸗, ⲝⲟⲟⲣⲉ† (ⲉⲃⲟⲗ) *scatter, disperse, hinder*; m. *scattering, dissolution*

ⲝⲣⲟ [ⲝⲣⲱ], ϭⲣⲟ, ⲝⲣⲁⲉⲓⲧ† *be strong, conquer*; m. *victory, strength*

 ⲁⲧⲝⲣⲟ ⲉⲣⲟ⸗ *unconquerable*

 ⲝⲟⲟⲣ† *be strong†, bold†*

 ⲝⲱⲱⲣⲉ [ⲝⲱⲣⲉ] m. *strong, mighty*

ⲝⲱⲣⲙ̄ *point, hint, beckon*

ⲝⲱⲣⲙ̄ *drive, ride*

ⲝⲱⲣⲡ *stumble, trip*

 ⲝⲣⲟⲡ [ⲝⲣⲁⲡ] m. *obstacle*

 †ⲝⲣⲟⲡ *trip up*

 ⲝⲓⲝⲣⲟⲡ *stumble*

[ⲝⲱⲣⲝ] v. ϭⲱⲣϭ *inhabit*

ⲝⲟⲉⲓⲥ, ⲝ̄ⲥ̄, [ⲝⲁⲉⲓⲥ, ⲝⲉⲥ-], pl. ⲝⲓⲥⲟⲟⲩ m. *lord, master*

ⲝⲓⲥⲉ, ⲝⲉⲥⲧ-, ⲝⲁⲥⲧ⸗, ⲝⲟⲥⲉ† [ⲝⲁⲥⲉ†], p.c. ⲝⲁⲥⲓ- *raise up, elevate, exalt, be high†*; m. *height*

 ⲝⲓⲥⲉ ⲛ̄ϩⲏⲧ *be vain, arrogant*

ⲝⲓⲥⲉ f. *back, spine*

ⲝⲓⲧ⸗ v. ⲝⲓ *receive*

ⲝⲟⲉⲓⲧ, ⲝⲓⲧ- m. *olive tree, olive*

ⲝⲁⲧⲉ [ⲝⲉⲧⲉ], ⲝⲟⲧⲉ† *ripen*

ⲝⲱⲧⲉ, ⲝⲉⲧ-, ⲝⲟⲧ⸗ *pierce, penetrate*

[ⲝⲱⲧⲉ] v. ϭⲱⲧ *drinking trough*

ⲝⲧⲟ, ϣⲧⲟ, ⲝⲧⲉ-, ⲝⲧⲟ⸗, ϣⲧⲟ⸗, ⲝⲧⲏⲩ†, ϣⲧⲏⲩ† *lay down, lying† down*

ⲝⲁⲧϥⲉ, ⲝⲁⲧⲃⲉ m. *reptile*

ⲝⲟⲟⲩ, ⲝⲁⲩ, ⲝⲉⲩ-, ⲝⲟⲟⲩ⸗ *send*

ⲝⲓⲟⲩⲉ *steal, rob*; m. *theft*

 ⲛ̄ⲝⲓⲟⲩⲉ *stealthily*

 ⲣⲉϥⲝⲓⲟⲩⲉ m. *thief*

ϫⲟⲟⲩⲧ   n. *inferior, worthless, rejected person* or *thing*

ϫⲟⲩⲱⲧ, f. ϫⲟⲩⲱⲧⲉ, ϫⲟⲩⲧ-   *twenty*

[ϫⲱϣ   *pour out*; m. *confusion*]

ϫⲁϥ   m. *frost*

ϫⲟϥⲧⲛ̄ inⲛ̄ϫⲟϥⲧⲛ̄   *headlong*

ϫⲟϥϫϥ, ϫⲟⲃϫⲃ̄, ϫⲉϥϫⲱϥ⸗   *burn, cook*

ϫⲱϩ, ϫⲉϩ-, ϫⲏϩ†   *touch*

ϫⲱϩ, ϫⲉϩ-, ϫⲁϩ⸗, ϫⲏϩ†   *smear, anoint*

ϫⲟⲩϩⲉ   *limp*

ϫⲱϩⲙ̄ [ϫⲱϩⲙⲉ], ϫⲉϩⲙ̄-, ϫⲁϩⲙ⸗ [ϫⲟϩⲙ⸗], ϫⲁϩⲙ̄†   *be unclean, defiled,*
    defile, pollute; m. *pollution, dirtiness*

ϫⲁϩϫϩ, ϭⲟϩϫϩ, ϭⲁϩϭϩ   *beat, gnash*; m. *beating, gnashing*

ϫⲁϫ   m. *sparrow*

ϫⲱϫ, ϫⲱ⸗   m. *head* (cf. ϫⲱ⸗)

    ⲁⲛϫⲱϫ   m. *chief, commander*

ϫⲁϫⲉ, ϫⲁϫⲱⲧ   *be hard, rough*

ϫⲁϫⲉ, pl. ϫⲓϫⲉⲉⲅⲉ   m.f. *enemy*

ϫⲓϫⲱⲓ   n. *hairlock*

    name of fourth-century monk (transliterated Σισώης)

[ϫⲟⲩϫⲟⲩ   *twitter,* cf. ϫⲁϫ]

[ϫⲁϭⲏ, ϭⲁϫⲏ   f. *left hand*]

ϫⲱϭⲉ, ϫⲟϭ⸗, ϫⲏϭ†   *dye, stain*

    ϫⲏϭⲉ   m. *purple dye, purple cloth, purple*

    ⲥⲁⲛ̄ϫⲏϭⲉ   m. *dealer in purple cloth*

[ϫϭⲓⲧ] v. ϣϫⲓⲧ   *dyer*

6
called ϭⲓⲙⲁ   transliterated č

6 sometimes interchanges with ϫ, ⲕ or ⲅ

ϭⲁⲓⲟ, ϭⲁⲓⲉ v. ⲧϭⲁⲓⲟ   *condemn*

ϭⲉ   *then, therefore, so, thus, again,* neg. *no longer*

ϭⲉ v. ⲕⲉ   *another*

ϭⲓⲉ   m. male *goat*

ϭⲱ, ϭⲉⲉⲧ†   *continue, keep, stop, quit, remain, remaining†, stay†*

[ϭⲓⲃⲉ] v. ⲉⲕⲓⲃⲉ   *breast*

ϭⲱⲱⲃⲉ, ϭⲱⲃⲉ, ϭⲃ̄-   f. *leaf*

    ϭⲃ̄ϣⲁ   pl. *nostrils*

ϭⲃⲟⲓ   m. *arm*

ϭⲃ̄ⲃⲉ, ϭⲟⲟⲃ†, p.c. ϭⲁⲃ-   *be weak*

    ϭⲱⲃ   m. *weakling*

    ⲙⲛ̄ⲧϭⲱⲃ   f. *weakness*

    ϭⲁⲃϩⲏⲧ   *be afraid*; m. *coward*

[ϭⲃⲟⲩⲣ] v. ϩⲃⲟⲩⲣ   *left hand*

[ϭⲏⲗ   m. *cry*

    ⲁϣϭⲏⲗ   *cry, shout*]

ϭⲟⲗ   m. *lie, liar*

    ϫⲓϭⲟⲗ, ϫⲉϭⲟⲗ   *tell a lie* (ϫⲱ)

[ϭⲁⲗⲙⲉ] m. *denier of truth*

ϭⲱⲗ, ϭⲝ-, ϭⲟⲗ⸗ *collect, gather*

ϭⲱⲗ, ϭⲝ-, ϭⲟⲗ⸗, ϭⲏⲗ† *return, roll back*
 ϭⲱⲗ ⲉⲃⲟⲗ *return, turn back*

ϭⲁⲗⲉ, pl. ϭⲁⲗⲉⲉⲩ n. *lame person, handicapped person*

ϭⲟⲓⲗⲉ, ⲕⲟⲓⲗⲉ, ϭⲁⲗⲉ-, ϭⲁⲗⲱⲱ⸗, ϭⲁⲗⲱⲟⲩ†, ϭⲁⲗⲏⲩⲧ† [ϭⲉⲗⲓⲧ†] *dwell, visit*
 ⲣⲙⲛϭⲟⲉⲓⲗⲉ m. *stranger, visitor*

ϭⲟⲓⲗⲉ, ϭⲁⲗⲉ- ⲕⲁⲗⲉ-, ϭⲁⲗⲱ⸗, ϭⲁⲗⲱⲟⲩ†, ϭⲁⲗⲏⲟⲩ† *deposit, entrust;*
 m. *deposit*

ϭⲱⲱⲗⲉ, ϭⲉⲗⲉ-, ϭⲟⲟⲗ⸗, ϭⲟⲟⲗⲉⲧ† [ϭⲁⲗⲉⲧ†] *clothe, cover*

ϭⲗⲟ [ϭⲗⲁ] m. *vanity, illusion*

ϭⲗⲓⲗ m. *burnt offering*

ϭⲝⲙ n. *sticks, twigs*

[ϭⲗⲁⲙ, ϭⲗⲟⲙ (v. ⲕⲱⲗⲉⲙ) *hurry;* m. *hurry*
 ⲛϭⲗⲟⲙ *quickly*]

ϭⲝⲙⲁⲓ [ϭⲝⲙⲉⲉⲓ] m. *jar*

ϭⲗⲟⲙⲗⲙ, ϭⲗⲙ̄ⲗⲱⲙ⸗, ϭⲗⲙ̄ⲗⲱⲙⲧ†, ϭⲗⲙ̄ⲗⲟⲙⲧ† *be twisted, combined, embrace;*
 m. *combination*

ϭⲱⲗⲡ, ϭⲝⲡ-, ϭⲟⲗⲡ⸗ [ϭⲁⲗⲡ⸗], ϭⲟⲗⲡ† [ϭⲁⲗⲉⲡⲧ†] (ⲉⲃⲟⲗ) *uncover, open,*
 reveal; m. *revelation*

ϭⲗⲱⲧ, pl. ϭⲗⲟⲟⲧⲉ [ϭⲗⲁⲧⲉ] m.f. *kidney*

ϭⲱⲗϫ, ϫⲱⲗϭ, ϭⲝϫ-, ϫⲉⲗⲉϫ-, ϭⲟⲗϫ⸗, ϭⲟⲗϭ⸗, ϭⲟⲗϫⲧ† *entangle, ensnare,*
 cling, adhere
 [ϭⲁⲗⲉⲥ f. *snare, enclosure*]

ϭⲱⲗϫ v. ⲕⲱⲗϫ *bend*

ϭⲗⲟϭ m. *bed, dining couch, stretcher, bier*

ϭⲙ̄- v. ϭⲓⲛⲉ

ϭⲟⲙ [ϭⲁⲙ] f. *power, strength, force*
 ⲁⲧϭⲟⲙ *powerless, unable*
 ⲟⲩⲛ̄(ϣ)ϭⲟⲙ ⲙ̄ⲙⲟ⸗ *be possible for one*
 ⲙⲛ̄(ϣ)ϭⲟⲙ ⲙ̄ⲙⲟ⸗ *be impossible for one*
 (ϣ)ϭⲙ̄ϭⲟⲙ *be strong, able* (ϣ-, ϭⲓⲛⲉ)

ϭⲱⲙ, pl. ϭⲟⲟⲙ m. *field, garden, property*
 ϭⲙⲉ m. *gardener*

ϭⲱⲱⲙⲉ, ϭⲉⲙⲉ-, ϭⲟⲟⲙⲉⲧ† *twist, pervert, crooked†;* m. *perversion*

ϭⲁⲙⲟⲩⲗ m.f. *camel*

ϭⲟⲙϭⲙ̄ [ϭⲁⲙϭⲙ̄], ϭⲙ̄ϭⲱⲙ⸗ *touch, grope*

ϭⲓⲛ-, ϭⲛ̄- [ϭⲓ-] *prefix forming fem. nouns of action*

ϭⲓⲛⲉ, ϭⲛ̄-, ϭⲙ̄-, ϭⲛ̄ⲧ⸗ *find;* m. *discovery*

ϭⲓⲛⲙⲟⲩⲧ, ϭⲓⲙⲟⲩⲧ f. *the Pleiades*

ϭⲛⲟⲛ, ϭⲏⲛ†, ϭⲟⲛ† *be soft, weak;* m. *softness*
 ϭⲟⲛ, ϭⲱⲛ *soft*

ϭⲟⲛⲥ n. *violence*
 ϫⲓⲛϭⲟⲛⲥ *mistreat, hurt;* m. *violence, injustice*

ϭⲱⲛⲧ, ϭⲟⲛⲧ† [ϭⲁⲛⲧ†] *be angry;* m. *anger*
 ϭⲛⲁⲧ *be angry*

ϭⲁⲛⲁϩ m. *maimed person*

ϭⲓⲛϭⲱⲣ m. *talent*

ϭⲟⲡ f. *sole* of the foot, *foot*

ϭⲉⲡⲏ *hurry*
 ϩⲛⲟⲩϭⲉⲡⲏ *quickly*
ϭⲏⲡⲉ [ⲕⲏⲡⲉ] f. *cloud*
ϭⲟⲡⲉ, ϭⲟⲡ, ϭⲁⲡⲉ m.f. *little bit, few*
ϭⲱⲡⲉ, ϭⲉⲡ-, ϭⲟⲡ⸗, ϭⲏⲡⲧ *catch, take*
ϭⲁⲡⲓⲭⲉ m.f. *measure*
ϭⲣⲏ *dig*
ϭⲣⲟ v. ϫⲣⲟ *be strong*
ϭⲉⲣⲱⲃ m. *staff, rod*
ϭⲣⲟⲟⲙⲡⲉ, ϭⲣⲟⲙⲡⲉ m.f. *dove*
 ϭⲣⲙ̄ⲡϣⲁⲛ f. *turtledove*
ϭⲣⲏⲡⲉ f. *crown, sceptre*
ϭⲱⲣϩ m. *night*
ϭⲣⲱϩ m. *want, need*
ϭⲟⲣϫ m. *dirt, filth*
ϭⲱⲣϭ, ϭⲟⲣϭⲧ *hunt*
 ϭⲱⲣϭⲥ f. *trap*
 ϭⲉⲣⲏϭ m. *hunter*
ϭⲱⲣϭ *prepare, provide;* m. *contents, mixture*
ϭⲱⲣϭ [ϫⲱⲣϫ] *inhabit, dwell*
ϭⲣⲟϭ [ϭⲣⲁϭ], ϭⲣⲟⲟϭ, pl. ϭⲣⲱⲱϭ m. *seed*
ϭⲟⲥ, ⲕⲁⲥ, ϭⲓⲥ-, ϭⲉⲥ- *half*
ϭⲟⲥⲙ̄ m. *storm*
ϭⲟⲥϭⲥ *dance*
ϭⲉⲉⲧⲧ *remaining* v. ϭⲱ
ϭⲟⲧ f. *size, age, form*
ϭⲱⲧ [ϫⲱⲧⲉ] f. *drinking trough*
ϭⲱⲧⲡ, ϭⲉⲧⲡ-, ϭⲟⲧⲡ⸗, ϭⲟⲧⲡⲧ *defeat, be defeated, overcome;*
 m. *discouragement*
ϭⲱⲧϩ *wound, pierce;* m. *hole*
ϭⲱⲟⲩ, ϭⲟⲟⲩ⸗, ϭⲏⲩⲧ *make narrow*
ϭⲱⲟⲩ (ⲉⲃⲟⲗ) *put out to sea, sail*
ϭⲁⲟⲩⲟⲛ [ϭⲁⲩⲁⲛ, pl. ϭⲁⲟⲩⲟⲛⲉ] m.f. *slave, servant*
ϭⲟⲟⲩⲛⲉ f. *haircloth, gunnysack*
ϭⲱⲟⲩϭ, ϭⲟⲟⲩϭⲧ *be crooked*
ϭⲱϣⲧ, ϭⲟϣⲧⲧ [ϭⲁϣⲧⲧ] *look, stare, watch*
 ϭⲱϣⲧ ⲛ̄ⲥⲁ-, ⲛ̄ⲥⲱ⸗ *look at, see*
 ϭⲱϣⲧ ⲉⲃⲟⲗ, ⲉⲃⲟⲗ ϩⲏⲧ⸗ *look toward, expect*
ϭⲟϣϭⲱ, ϭⲉϣϭⲱϣ⸗, ϭⲉϣϭⲱϣⲧ *sprinkle;* m. *sprinkling*
ϭϩⲟⲥ, ϭⲟϩⲥⲉ, ϭⲁϩⲥⲉ f. *gazelle*
ϭⲟϩϫϩ, ϭⲁϩϭϩ v. ϫⲁϩϫϩ *beat*
ϭⲓϫ f. *hand*
[ϭⲁϫⲏ v. ϫⲁϭⲏ *left hand*]
ϭⲱⲱϫⲉ, ϭⲱϫⲉ, ϫⲉϫ-, ϭⲟϫϩ⸗, ϭⲟⲟϫⲉⲧ, p.c. ϭⲁⲁϫⲉ- *cut*
 ϭⲱϫⲉ, ϭⲉϫ-, ϭⲏϫⲧ *dig*
ϭⲱϫⲃ, ϭⲱϫϥ, ϭⲟϫⲃⲧ [ϭⲁϫⲃⲧ, ϭⲁϫϥⲧ] *be small, be insignificant, lessen;*
 m. *inferiority*
[ϭⲉϫⲙ̄ in ⲁⲧϫⲓϭⲉϫⲙ̄ *untraceable*]
ϭⲟϫϭϫ, ϭⲉϫϭⲟϫⲧⲧ *slice, hit, slaughter*

ϭⲱϭ,ϭⲟϭⲁ,ϭⲏϭⲧ *roast, bake*
   ϭⲁⲁϭⲉ m.f. *loaf*

✝

called ✝ transliterated *ti*

✝ treated as ⲧⲓ
✝ for def. art. sing. fem. before Gk. words with initial ⲉⲓ-,
   e.g., ✝ⲣⲏⲛⲏ ⲛⲏⲧⲛ̄ *peace to you*

Lightning Source UK Ltd.
Milton Keynes UK
UKHW042101080119
335203UK00001B/69/P